Thirty Seconds to Air

Thirty Seconds

to Air

A Field Reporter's
Guide to Live
Television Reporting

Bob Arya

 Iowa State University Press *Ames*

Bob Arya is an experienced, award-winning television reporter who is currently working in the Chicago area. He has also worked as a news anchor and as an on-air radio personality. He holds a B.S. in mass communications/broadcast journalism from Illinois State University.

Iowa State University Press
2121 South State Avenue, Ames, Iowa 50014

Orders: 1-800-862-6657
Office: 1-515-292-0140
Fax: 1-515-292-3348
Web site: www.isupress.edu

The A&E logo is a trademark of A&E Television Networks and is provided courtesy of A&E Network.

Authorization to photocopy items for internal or personal use, or the internal or personal use of specific clients, is granted by Iowa State University Press, provided that the base fee of $.10 per copy is paid directly to the Copyright Clearance Center, 222 Rosewood Drive, Danvers, MA 01923. For those organizations that have been granted a photocopy license by CCC, a separate system of payments has been arranged. The fee code for users of the Transactional Reporting Service is 0-8138-2579-2/99 $.10.

♾ Printed on acid-free paper in the United States of America

First edition, 1999

Library of Congress Cataloging-in-Publication Data

Arya, Bob
    Thirty seconds to air : a field reporter's guide to live television reporting / Bob Arya.
        p.   cm.
    Includes bibliographical references.
    ISBN 0-8138-2579-2
    1. Television broadcasting of news. 2. Reporters and reporting.
    I. Title. II. Title: Thirty seconds to air.
    PN4784.T4A79   1999
    070.1'95—dc21   99–14529

The last digit is the print number: 9   8   7   6   5   4   3   2

This book is dedicated with love to my wife Terry, my best friend and partner for life. To my mother and father—Mano and Shelia—who gave me the tools, the love, and the support to make it in life. To my brother, Kevin, and my sisters, Jacki and Raj. To my wonderful in-laws, Bob, Sharon, Sue, Sylvia, Connie, Tim, Dawn, Tricia, Steve, Todd, Kaitlyn, Katie, and Tim.

Contents

Foreword

Forty years ago, the best preparation for a live television report was a job in radio. Radio had entertained us during the Depression, carried us through World War II, and by the mid-fifties still held our respect when compared with the upstart newcomer called television. The names in radio news sounded like Founding Fathers: Murrow, Sevareid, Shirer, Collingwood, Hottelet, Kaltenborn, Thomas. Their eyes were our eyes to the history-making events that changed the world.

They earned the listeners' respect not because they had deep voices or handsome faces but because they were great writers. Their words were chosen and their sentences structured to tell a story that communicated facts, yes. But it also held the listener with its narrative thread, which in most cases was carefully crafted at a typewriter long before the words were read into a microphone.

Edward R. Murrow spoke of an "orchestrated hell" when he described the sight of bombs hitting a German city. He asked us to listen to footsteps on the sidewalk outside a bomb shelter during the air raids over London. The feeling of *live* reporting transported us there to experience the danger. What the listener did not realize is that Murrow had composed it carefully on paper.

Good writing organizes facts into an understandable form and locks the writer's brain into gear. No presentation can be saved if the story cannot be understood.

Unfortunately, today's live broadcasts leave little time for writing those beautiful word pictures for posterity. And while Murrow's spontaneous observations followed a script, the demands of today's television news business hardly allow the reporter to jot down a few notes much less read them on the air while looking into the camera.

Yet there is much we can learn from the "Founding Fathers."

First, good writing separates the memorable report from the also-ran. Good looks and voice can carry a young reporter through a nice career, but I doubt that anyone achieves greatness in this business without being able to write a good sentence.

Second, the key is preparation. It can compensate for inexperience. I'm talking about more than reading a few clips before leaving the studio for a story. If you're in the news business, preparation is a lifestyle. Your time clock never turns off. If you're not soaking up every bit of information that flows from the various sources that affect your beat, you should be seeking another line of work. You're the opposite of an archaeologist. Instead of peeling back the sands of time to discover an ancient fossil, a reporter is adding those layers every day, concentrating on the community events that are big enough to mark the date for history.

An editor or producer should look back at the end of the day and wonder, "Did we serve our viewers well today? Did we accurately explain those events that would be chosen for a time capsule of this day, events that were meaningful to the lives of those who live in this community?"

And perhaps the most important lesson: Journalists serve the viewer or reader first, the stockholders second.

Back to the point. The television reporter facing a live shot probably won't have time for a trip to the film library or a rummage through old scripts. The only files that you can call upon are those in your own head. The facts that you absorbed from a radio newscast or quick perusal of *The New York Times* will serve you well eight hours later. That's preparation. If you have time to research a particular story, consider yourself lucky.

Your brain is also a workbench where you'll be organizing facts into a story, sometimes while the camera is rolling. Here are a few tips I've learned, which can be applied to either long-form or live situations.

The television viewer can't go back and re-view a report like a newspaper; so it has to be understood the first time around. That means the story must be simple—no tricks—and must lead the viewer through a narrative that has a beginning, a middle, and an end.

Ancient storytellers conveyed the tribe's customs and history by oral tradition before they had a written language. Imagine that challenge! What kind of delivery system would you use if you had to tell a child something she could never forget? They used stories. The *story* organizes facts into images that are relevant to their lives. These accounts could be easily remembered in the story form.

Like the ancient craft of storytelling, television has no written language which a viewer can peruse. We in the field communicate with pictures and spoken words, which must flow logically from introduction to conclusion. Our goal is to create a story that links pictures and words together in a seamless flow, beginning to end. The story will provide the structure. The best summation of what goes into that structure is the journalist's credo: Who did What? When and Where did it occur and How?

It's painfully simple, isn't it? But after forty years in this business, I've found that the best reporters never forget the basic rules. They build great careers finding imaginative ways to assemble those simple elements. They never seem to lose the fun that comes with putting thoughts and images together in a story.

Most of the problems arise when a reporter no longer finds joy in matching the facts to the basic rules of story-telling. Elements are omitted; shortcuts are taken. The sloppy or lazy habits that form undermine a career. The reasons behind such a slide are many, and trying to trace the ups and downs of a career would better fill a psychology book than this one.

If your early years are spent slavishly experimenting with a formula for good writing, it will become an unconscious expression of your thoughts—how you tell a joke, how you tell your daughter a bedtime story. Your thoughts will begin to sort themselves out logically. You will have learned the secret. It will serve you well throughout your career. That is, when you can invisibly and unconsciously apply this structure to telling a story, you're ready for the difficult task of live television. It's difficult because you'll have to do it in your head, often at the same time that you are speaking the words.

Briefly, there are several kinds of live reporting: a descriptive on-the-scene report of a live event; wall-to-wall coverage of a breaking story—from the anchor's slot; and a *live shot* within a newscast. You're lucky. Bob Arya is going to provide what none of us had in the early days: a touchstone guide that could save a lot of heartaches in your first experiences.

On the other hand, *going live* is like learning to swim. Despite the best instruction, sooner or later you have to get into the water. And you will find that it is a world in which you have to build your own experiences.

Let's touch briefly on the *live anchor experience*. You are sitting at an anchor desk when the story breaks. Without warning, you are suddenly "directing traffic" around you, that is, integrating reporters into the broadcast, interviewing experts at the scene of a disaster to help understand the context of what is happening—all the time accumulating new facts that layer one on top of the other as a story develops. The anchor must keep track of it all. I have found it both exhilarating when the information is flowing fast and accurately and depressing when you seem to be just filling time until the next development occurs. You are only as good as the people behind you.

The entire newsroom should know what to do when the decision is made to go live. Each person should have a role either gathering information and channeling it to the anchor desk or helping to produce visuals on the air. Too often I've looked across the newsroom to see staff members standing in front of a television set to get their information. They were watching me as if there were a magic source that appeared on the desk in front of me. I shouted, "That's funny. I get my information from you! If none of us are gathering facts, let's watch the competition."

If you're fortunate enough to be in the right place at the right time to describe an event happening before your eyes, it might help to resist being drawn into the emotion of the moment. Remember, unless you can prevent injury to life or limb by your personal actions, accurately communicating the story to those who can effectively do something will accomplish far more than your solitary effort. In most cases, you are part of a system. Your job is to communicate that the tree is down, not to operate the chain saw.

However, there are times when a little emotion is necessary. My formative experience in broadcasting came during such a situation in Topeka, Kansas, June 8, 1966. I was twenty-six at the time. I called back in front of a studio camera to give a warning about high winds associated with a cold front moving across the Flint Hills west of the Capitol. While I was referring to my notes during this brief on-camera appearance, an off-camera voice penetrated the studio's silence telling me that a tornado had been sighted by our cameraman on the city's southwestern edge. I gave our standard tornado warning and filled about thirty more seconds before getting the shock of my life: The twister had wiped out a huge apartment complex and was heading straight for the downtown section. In a flash I could see the mental images of streets lined with houses in the path of the storm with families comfortably watching television—*me*. I felt the inner hysteria that comes when you face life or death decisions. In this case, doing my job of communicating danger could either get people to their basements or waste valuable seconds. With voice choking, I said, "For

God's sake, take cover!" Over the top? Not that time. It carried the necessary passion to convince viewers that this was not just another "warning"—they must head for their basements. Both WIBW-TV and its radio counterpart simulcasted for twenty-four hours, becoming players in the experience of sounding an alarm and then helping rescue efforts. I think that the feelings of serving our viewers over those twenty-four hours was the most rewarding experience of my forty years in broadcasting. The staffs gave the peak efforts of their careers. Lives were at stake.

From that defining moment, I have regarded my profession with a spiritual respect. I was fortunate to see firsthand what *live* television could achieve.

This book will help you appreciate that same potential and prepare you for building a set of your own experiences. I sincerely hope that you find it as thrilling as I have.

Bill Kurtis
President, Kurtis Productions
Host, A&E Documentaries

Introduction

There is no skill more important to a television news reporter than the ability to excel at live television. Solid live reporting skills separate the best from the rest of the pack in this field. Such skills are critical in landing a job and moving up in the business. Years ago, a news director would look at a resume tape and evaluate the candidate's credibility on camera, look of confidence, and writing skills. In the last decade things have changed. When most news directors look at a resume tape they still are evaluating the aforementioned criteria, but they are focusing as much also on how well the reporter handles himself or herself in live news situations. Most news directors will tell you that live ability makes a big difference when it comes to hiring. If you are a reporter with credibility, good writing skills, and a solid live presentation, you will be in a great position to land that job!

Live television is an art form. A flawless live shot under difficult circumstances is one of the most thrilling experiences a reporter can hope to have. Live television stands out. It is the challenge of bringing viewers the latest information available on a story in a short period of time. It is clearing hurdles, both natural and created, to beat deadlines. It is to think faster and work harder and smarter.

All you need do is watch your local news to see the best and the worst of live television reporting. It is easy to spot those journalists whose live skills are polished and credible. It is easier to pick out those who are uncomfortable and awkward.

Mastering the art of live television is not easy. This field is not for everyone. To be truly good at live television, you must do more than talk clearly and look good. Live television requires a journalist to draw from his or her life experiences. A good live reporter is a very good news writer. The best in this business are those that operate at a higher level. Live television demands self-control, discipline, and sharp focus.

A good live television reporter is one who can really tell a story in an accurate, clear, and concise fashion while adding insight and detail, and doing so under duress at times. So what separates the good live reporters from the rest? You will find it has a lot less to do with sheer talent than it does with preparation and practice.

This book is a unique teaching tool on the topic of live television news reporting. It is unique because, until now, a book solely devoted to this topic did not exist in this form. Most broadcast journalism textbooks that discuss live television do so in a chapter or a few pages and are very general in scope. This textbook goes beyond the basics of live reporting. It is a manual for success. Here we will explore the techniques reporters use to prepare for and present a live report. We will look at what can and will go wrong with live presentations. The legal, ethical, technical, and very personal issues tied to live television news reporting will all be discussed. Practice material and tips on how to use it are also included.

The material presented here draws from the experiences of those who are at the top of their games in live television news around the country. In failure, there is often success. Many of the tips and techniques that are mentioned in this book come from those who have been there and, through trial and error, have discovered ways to sharpen their live skills.

This book is designed to help you build a solid foundation for an extremely rewarding career. It is a real-life teaching aid that will show you what it takes to be prepared and confident when the producer's voice comes through your earpiece and gives you the signal: "Thirty Seconds to Air."

Acknowledgments

Thanks to the many people without whose help this book would not have been possible. I give special thanks to all my coworkers in Chicago and to Jim Disch, news director. Thanks also to the Tribune Company and *The Chicago Tribune*.

I would also like to thank the following people and organizations for all of their help in bringing this book together: Norm Goldstein, director of APN Special Projects with the Associated Press; Maggie Balough, acting director of the Society of Professional Journalists (SPJ); the Radio-Television News Directors Association (RTNDA); Estee Portnoy and Rand Sacks with F.A.M.E., Inc.; Michael Jordan, NIKE, Inc., and Kate Bowden, NIKE's advertising and business affairs coordinator; and Northwestern University's Medil School of Journalism and the head of its Broadcast Program, Patricia Dean. Thanks also to Vernon A. Stone, Missouri School of Journalism; Jay Groves and John Fisk from Illinois State University; Sheldon Ripson; Frank Vascellaro; David Rosenberg; Jason Walle; Derrick Robinson; Steve Vogel; Kevin and Laurie Uttich; and attorneys Don Craven and Joe Thornton; Cris Wyatt; Jeri Porter; and Bill Kurtis of A&E Television Networks.

My sincere thanks as well to Iowa State University Press and its Acquisitions Project Manager, Judi Brown, for having faith in this project and its author and for making a dream a reality.

Bob Arya

Thirty Seconds to Air

1

The Basics

Every reporter remembers that first professional live shot. It is a moment that brings together all of the hopes of a young reporter, and it is a true test of how well prepared he or she is to begin a career in live television news reporting. Unfortunately, for many it is also a moment they would like to forget. As a cub reporter, the first live shot is a chance to show your news director and the veteran field generals that you have what it takes to make it. A successful first live shot is a true landmark. It is the beginning of the solid foundation of confidence upon which a successful career can be built. A blown first live shot, on the other hand, can be downright devastating. In some cases, it can be the beginning of the end of a career.

As you will learn, there are many things that can happen to disrupt a live shot or destroy it altogether. What is important is the ability to recognize these obstacles in advance and learn to work with or around them. It is also very important to be able to handle stressful situations that develop and put everything into perspective. A firm understanding of the basics of live television news is the key to success.

Overcoming Anxiety

One of the biggest hurdles to success in live television reporting is fear. It is natural to experience a certain level of anxiety in any job, but in live television news, the level of anxiety can be exceptionally high. News in and of itself is a stressful business: There are always deadlines right around the corner, and it never feels as if you have enough time to get what you need or want. Finding ways to cope with stress and learning to use fear as a motivator are essential to building confidence in this field.

In live television news, you have one chance to get it right. When you present your story, your facts must be accurate, your look must be appropriate, your delivery must be confident and credible. You must also be concise and thorough at the same time. In addition to all this, you often must deliver your presentation under duress. It is no wonder many young reporters, and even some veterans, find themselves battling anxious moments just prior to live shots.

While interviewing a number of successful television news reporters for this book, I came up with a list of the three most common reasons for the anxiety that sometimes precedes a live television news event. The first and easiest to understand is the basic fear of failure; the second is fear of failing in the eyes of one's peers; and the third is fear of letting the public down.

Fear of Failure

Most of us have at one time or another in our lives wanted to do something, but were held back by the fear that we might fail in the attempt. Some people are much better than others at telling jokes. They are usually the life of the party when around friends. However, many of these same people remain in their seats during open mike night at the local comedy club. They watch others telling their jokes, but can't bring themselves to step up to the microphone and perform. Why? Because they fear failure. Nothing would be more embarrassing than getting up and telling a joke only to hear a room full of silence when the punch line is delivered.

As a live television news reporter, you are generally not trying to evoke laughter with your presentation, but there is fear that you might. We have all seen reporters botch live shots. In many of these cases the reporter freezes on air after forgetting what he or she is talking about. This is known as the "deer in the headlights" syndrome. Reporters are also known to chew on their tongues from time to time and end up saying things that make no sense whatsoever.

In live television, when you make a mistake on air, every second starts to feel like an eternity. Many young reporters are too concerned about making mistakes. They tend to think about what friends and family members who might be watching will think of them if they mess up. This fear of failure can become a self-fulfilling prophecy. If you are not focused and are afraid that you are going to screw up, odds are that you will. Many young reporters are anxious before live shots and fail to prepare properly. That is why the level of anxiety goes through the roof when the reporter is given a thirty-second cue.

Fear of Failing in front of Peers

Young reporters have a lot to prove to themselves, to their bosses, and to their peers. In many cases, a mistake may not be noticed by the average viewer, but you can bet that any mistake you make will be recognized by your news director, by reporters at your station, and by your peers at competing stations. We all want to be recognized for good work. In television news, two things are very important—credibility and respect. A reporter who consistently fails to deliver good live reports runs the risk of losing both in the eyes of others in the field. This becomes very important when building a career. If you get a reputation for lackluster live shots, you may not be selected for the best stories. In the long term, consistently poor live performances may limit your ability to move up and on in this career.

Fear of Failing the Public

There are other reporters who fear letting the public down with a poor performance. When you decide to become a television news reporter, you are undertaking an awesome responsibility. Freedom of the press (and, by extension, other reporting media) is one of the foundations upon which this country is built. You are often reporting on weighty issues that can or will have a significant impact on a large segment of your viewership.

In cases of emergency, natural or otherwise, there can be a lot at stake. The nature of the subject matter and the relative inexperience of the reporter can add to the level of anxiety already present. There are concerns about reporting erroneous information in these cases. If a reporter makes a mistake while live and does not rebound properly, there can be serious consequences. If you are dealing with controversial matters or with the reputation of some individual or group there also may be significant legal ramifications tied to your reporting.

No matter what the cause, fear can become a permanent obstacle to live performance if it is not managed properly. It is important to understand how fear and anxiety work to undermine your state of mind and ability to perform. Anxiety impacts your mind, your body, and your actions and behaviors. Physiologically, anxiety can increase your heartbeat, make you feel sick to the stomach, tighten your muscles, and make it difficult for you to breathe. These factors alone can make pulling off a successful live shot impossible before you are even on air.

The best way to combat fear is with knowledge and understanding. When you are comfortable with what is expected of you and what you need to do, situations that would otherwise be anxiety filled start to become exciting. Rookie or veteran, you can instantly reduce your level of anxiety by focusing on what you have to work with, what time constraints you are under, and what form your live report will take.

The Live Shot

Live shots can be brief and well scripted or, in the case of some breaking news events, free-form, no-holds-barred coverage. There are, however, some basic formats that live presentations take on regardless of the type of event you are covering. These formats include the wraparound, the live video/sound on tape (vo-sot) shot, and live video (vo) report, the scene scope, and the live interview. We will take a look at each basic format and discuss the best approach to a story given time constraints and the availability of material. First we must set the scene:

A fire has broken out at an apartment complex. Two people are dead, and several people are trapped in upper level units. Several dozen firefighters are on the scene. An extra alarm has been called to bring in more fire engines and manpower. Police have secured the scene. There are dozens of people on the perimeter set up by police. Some of these people are residents who escaped from their apartments. Others live in the building and arrived home to find the building ablaze. There are a number of other people on the scene from an adjacent building, and still more who are just curious onlookers who happened upon the scene. Heavy smoke is visible as are flames from a number of the units. It is a sunny afternoon, but the wind is blowing and gusting and the temperature is very cold and dropping.

The length and format of your live shot is generally determined by three major factors: time, availability of information or resources, and your role in the coverage. Time is a major factor in your choice of length and style of coverage. If you are arriving on the scene of this fire shortly before your newscast, odds are you will have to limit both the length and scope of your presentation. The show producer or executive producer may also place limits on the time you have to tell your story. In this case, it is a pretty good bet that you are the lead story and may be allowed additional time.

Availability of information or resources will also affect the length and style of your presentation. It may be that you are able to talk with witnesses, victims, police, fire officials, the Salvation Army, and whoever else is at the scene. In this case you have more sound and information than you will be able to use in your report. Conversely, if you are arriving late, you may not have time to seek out interviews right away; they will have to wait until you have concluded your initial live report.

The third major factor to consider in determining the length and scope of your presentation is your role in the coverage. It is not uncommon for stations to throw a lot of resources at a big story like this one. The team coverage approach usually means one reporter will get the lead—the nuts and bolts information. Other crews will be responsible for covering sidebar or related human interest angles to the story. The goal of team coverage is to give viewers all of the information they want and then some. If you are the lead reporter, you may have more time and additional resources for a longer and more comprehensive live report. If your assignment is to follow the lead with a live update on what local shelters are doing to prepare for the large number of expected homeless victims displaced by the fire, you may find yourself with less time and less to talk about.

The Wraparound

Once you know your role in coverage and can determine what resources you have to work with, you can then determine what form your live report will take. Let us begin with the best of all worlds. You arrive on the scene around four in the afternoon. Your live shot will lead off the six o'clock news. There is ample time to interview officials for the nuts and bolts information. You are looking for answers to where the fire might have started and how many people were in the building at the time. You are trying to determine what kind of manpower is needed to fight this fire and what obstacles firefighters face in trying to knock down flames and save lives. You are able to get interviews with witnesses at the scene, and from those who live in the building and managed to escape the flames with little more than the clothes on their backs. In short, you have a lot to work with and can craft a long form report to go along with your live report.

In this case, your live shot will likely take the form of a wraparound. A *wraparound* is just what it sounds like. The news anchor in studio will introduce the story to viewers then switch to the reporter in the field for more information. The reporter crafts a self-contained report or package, as it is called, then introduces that report. When the package is complete, the reporter will be back with the live conclusion to the piece. The pretaped package contains the reporter's narrative, natural sound breaks, interviews with officials, witnesses, residents, and of course, the best video of the fire and other relevant pictures. Here is what the process looks like:

> **Anchor:** Good evening ... two people are dead following a major fire on the city's northwest side. The blaze broke out around three thirty this afternoon at the Green View apartment complex. The fire is still not under control, and we understand that there are still some people trapped in their apartments. We go live now to reporter Amanda Houston who is on the scene with the latest. Amanda?

Reporter: As you can see behind me, firefighters are using ladders to try and rescue a couple of residents trapped on their third floor apartment balcony. Fire officials tell us they are the last of the residents to be removed from the building. It has been a very difficult situation for much of the afternoon. High winds and low water pressure are wreaking havoc with firefighters who are trying to extinguish this blaze.

The reporter's live introduction is complete when she utters the words "extinguish this blaze." This is known as a roll cue. At this point, the reporter's pretaped package is played back at the station. The piece runs about ninety seconds and contains information about the two individuals killed in the blaze along with sound bites from the fire department, witnesses, and a victim who lost everything in the fire. At the conclusion of the pretaped report, the reporter is back live on the scene with a few thoughts and possibly a question or two from the studio.

Reporter: A third fire company has been called in to assist in fighting the fire. The Salvation Army is here to help those displaced by the fire. The mayor says he is opening up two community centers that will be used as temporary shelters to aid those left homeless by the blaze. Reporting live from the scene, I'm Amanda Houston, back to you in the studio.

Anchor: Amanda, is there any clue at this point as to the cause of the fire?

Reporter: Fire officials have yet to pinpoint an exact cause, but they believe the fire began in a second floor unit. The state fire marshall's office is on scene to conduct a thorough investigation once the blaze is completely extinguished.

At this point, the anchor thanks the reporter for her report and moves on to the next story. The reporter and crew are then cleared to pursue additional interviews and video for a follow-up report to air at ten o'clock.

The Live Video/Sound on Tape Shot (vo-sot)

Arriving on the scene later may limit your ability to piece together such a comprehensive report for the six o'clock news. Arriving on the scene after five o'clock means you will have to work quicker with less material at your disposal. In a case like this, your presentation may take the form of a *live vo-sot*. This means you will incorporate video and natural sound (vo) from the fire with whatever sound on tape (sot) you are able to gather. The sot may be from a witness, a fire official, a victim, or an aid worker.

The presentation will differ from the wraparound in a couple of ways. First, it will likely be much shorter than the package. Second, it will have fewer support elements. However, the information will be basically the same, and the value of the presentation is not diminished. In this case, the reporter managed to interview the fire chief, and her photographer was able to shoot some video of the fire that he will edit. A segment of the interview lasting between fifteen seconds and a half minute will be cut—this will be the sound on tape (sot) used in the live report. The video will be edited to create the vo that will be played during the presentation. Here is how the live vo-sot might be structured.

Anchor: Good evening ... two people are dead following a major fire on the city's northwest side. The blaze broke out around three thirty this afternoon at the Green View apartment complex. The fire is still not under control and we understand that there are still some people trapped in their apartments. We go live now to reporter Amanda Houston who is on the scene with the latest. Amanda?

Reporter: As you can see behind me, firefighters are using ladders to try and rescue a couple of residents trapped on their third floor apartment balcony. Fire officials tell us they are the last of the residents to be removed from the building. It has been a very difficult situation for much of the afternoon. High winds and low water pressure are wreaking havoc with firefighters who are trying to extinguish the blaze.

The last three words, "extinguish the blaze," are the reporter's roll cue once again. This time though, there is no package to run. At this point, the video is rolled back at the station. The reporter continues reading her script. Viewers at home hear her words while they watch the pre-edited video from the fire scene. Ideally, what the reporter is saying and what the audience is seeing will go hand in hand. It is very important that reporters write to the pictures.

The reporter will continue with her narrative until she

reaches a predetermined point at which the sound on tape (sot) will be played. This predetermined point is another roll cue. When the reporter hits the second roll cue, the sot with the fire chief will be played. It will replace the fire video that viewers had been watching up to this point. Let's pick up the report from the first roll cue. The reporter is reading her script. Viewers are seeing pre-edited video from the scene.

Reporter: These pictures can give you some idea of how intense this fire is. At one point fire officials say flames were shooting as high as a hundred feet above the roof of the building. The two people that died in the blaze were killed after jumping from this third floor balcony. Firefighters from several area departments have been pouring tens of thousands of gallons of water on the fire trying to bring it under control. Officials say they are having difficulty getting enough water on the fire because high winds are blowing the water everywhere. The fire department is also concerned that the fire might spread at this point. The fear is that the winds will carry burning embers to adjacent buildings.

Here, the reporter has reached her second roll cue, "to adjacent buildings." At this point the fire video will end, and we will hear from the fire chief, who will expound upon the concern that the blaze may spread if not contained soon.

Fire Chief: We are doing all we can to keep water on areas of this building that are closest to others. We are also going to begin pouring water on the roofs and siding of other nearby buildings. That will help reduce the chance of spreading the fire to other units if burning embers land on them.

The reporter has been off camera since she hit her first roll cue. Her voice was heard as she read the script under the vo. The reporter stopped talking altogether when she hit the second roll cue which signaled the station to roll the sound on tape from the fire chief. At the end of the sot from the fire chief, the reporter will be back on camera for her live tag. The final three words of the fire chief's sot make up the out cue, or the end of the sound, and signal the reporter that it is her turn once again to begin speaking. At this point, as with the wraparound, the reporter continues on with the balance of the report.

Reporter: A third fire company has been called in to assist in fighting the fire. The Salvation Army is here to help those displaced by the fire. The mayor says he is opening up two community centers to aid those left homeless by the blaze. Reporting live from the scene, I'm Amanda Houston, back to you in the studio.

At this point, as with the longer wraparound, if there is time, the anchor will question the reporter about the story. In fact, in cases where the reporter's story is shorter, as with the vo-sot, it is possible there will be more time to fill and more questions and interaction.

Anchor: Amanda, is there any clue at this point as to the cause of the fire?

Reporter: Fire officials have yet to pinpoint the exact cause, but they believe the fire began in a second floor unit. The state fire marshall's office is on scene to conduct a thorough investigation once the blaze is completely extinguished.

Anchor: The apartment complex is in a busy portion of the city ... what impact is it having on street closings and rush hour traffic in the area?

Reporter: Fire officials have shut down North and South streets for several blocks. Traffic is being allowed on East Street at this point, but that too may be closed because the shifting winds are beginning to blow flaming debris in that direction. So it is quite a mess and likely will be for some time. The best advice is of course to steer clear of this area altogether. Back to you.

At this point, the anchor thanks the reporter for her report and moves on to the next story. The reporter and crew then go on to work the story for a later newscast, shooting additional video and interviews. You'll notice that in this case, two questions helped extend the length of the piece and bring out more of the story. It is important that the reporter and anchor be on the same page if there is to be a lot of interaction. The last thing you want to see is the anchor asking the reporter a question he or she cannot answer. This is where clear communication between the field and the newsroom becomes even more important.

The Live Video (vo) Shot

There will be occasions on which you will not have the time or opportunity to interview anyone at the scene about what is going until after your live shot. In cases like these, you have a couple of options. The first is a live vo report. The second is a scene scan. We'll begin with the live vo.

This time the reporter and crew arrive at the fire scene at five forty. Fire officials give you a little bit of basic information off camera but say they won't be available for on-camera comment for another hour. Unfortunately, your live location is removed from much of the action and many of the people you would otherwise be able to interview for your report. The only good news is that your photographer is able to get some great video. At this point, your resources are very limited, and your live report will likely be brief and lacking significant detail. What you do have is basic information your news desk back at the station has been able to gather by phone.

Your news director and producer determine at this point that a live vo is the best way to go. Simply put, the *live vo* presentation is the same as that of the live vo-sot, minus, of course, the sot with the fire chief.

Anchor: Good evening ... two people are dead following a major fire on the city's northwest side. The blaze broke out around three thirty this afternoon at the Green View apartment complex. The fire is still not under control and we understand that there are still some people trapped in their apartments. We go now live to reporter Amanda Houston who is on the scene with the latest.

Reporter: As you can see behind me, firefighters are using ladders to try and rescue a couple of residents trapped on their third floor apartment balcony. Fire officials tell us that they are the last of the residents to be removed from the building. It has been a very difficult situation for much of the afternoon. High winds and low water pressure are wreaking havoc with firefighters who are trying to extinguish this blaze.

That is of course the reporter's roll cue. The reporter continues with her narrative while the station rolls the pre-edited fire video that her photographer shot.

Reporter: These pictures can give you some idea of how intense the fire is. At one point fire officials say flames were shooting as high as a hundred feet above the roof of the building. The two people that died in the blaze were killed after jumping from this third floor balcony. Firefighters from several area departments have been pouring tens of thousands of gallons of water on the fire trying to bring it under control. Officials say they are having difficulty getting enough water on the fire because high winds are blowing the water everywhere. The fire department is also concerned that the fire might spread at this point. The fear is that the winds will carry burning embers to adjacent buildings.

This time the three words "to adjacent buildings" is not a roll cue; it is an out cue. Since there is no pretaped report or sot for the reporter to go to, the reporter re-appears on camera after reaching the out cue. Before wrapping up the report at this point, the reporter might want to offer some of the same information the sot would have related if the fire chief had had time to interview on camera.

Reporter: The fire chief told me that firefighters are now spraying the roofs and siding of adjacent buildings to cool them down and reduce the chance of fire in the event burning embers are blown onto the buildings. Meanwhile, a third fire company has been called in to assist in fighting the fire. The Salvation Army is here to help those displaced by the fire. The mayor says he is opening up two community centers that will be used as temporary shelters to aid those left homeless by the blaze. Reporting live from the scene, I'm Amanda Houston, back to you in the studio.

From here, the anchor can ask questions and the reporter can respond to the best of his or her ability for as long as is needed to tell the story and fill the time.

The Scene Scan Shot

When all else fails, there is the *scene scan*. This is a technique usually reserved for those stories for which there is no time to shoot video or interviews. In these cases you are best served by using your environment and live camera work (scanning the scene) to tell the story. This approach requires the reporter and photographer to be in sync with respect to what will be said and what will be shown.

Keeping with our fire at the apartment complex, the crew arrives about ten minutes before six o'clock. There is no time to shoot interviews, there is no time to shoot video. The photographer is helping to set up the live shot while the reporter compiles information from the newsdesk and combines it with some information gathered during a quick discussion with the fire chief, who is too busy to do any more. The reporter in this case must quickly and logically craft a story that will contain detail and use live camera work as the vo in this case. This is accomplished by discussing matters with the photographer. The reporter will do an introduction on camera, then the camera will move off of the reporter to an area or an object that the reporter will reference. In this type of live shot, the reporter must be very precise in what is being said and the photographer must be listening closely to what the reporter is saying so that the shot will match the narrative. The reporter may have to rely less on what he or she has scripted and more on powers of observation and the ability to ad-lib or go with the flow in a case like this. This is one of the real tests of how well a live television news reporter performs. It requires quick thinking, processing a lot of information in a short period of time, and teamwork. This is how such a live shot might look.

Anchor: Good evening ... two people are dead following a major fire on the city's northwest side. The blaze broke out around three thirty this afternoon at the Green View apartment complex. The fire is still not under control, and we understand that there are still some people trapped in their apartments. We go live now to reporter Amanda Houston who is on the scene with the latest. Amanda?

Reporter: As you can see behind me, firefighters are using ladders to try and rescue a couple of residents trapped on their third floor apartment balcony. Fire officials tell us they are the last residents to be removed from the building. It has been a very difficult situation for much of the afternoon. High winds and low water pressure are wreaking havoc with the firefighters who are trying to extinguish this blaze.

At this point, the reporter has reached what would normally be the roll cue. Since there is nothing to roll, however, it becomes a cue to the photographer to move the camera off the reporter and onto the scene. The reporter then uses the live picture as the vo. The reporter has decided not to follow her script word by word in this case; instead she follows an outline based on the original script. The photographer begins with a wide shot of the apartment building and begins to zoom in on the flames of the upper floors.

Reporter: As you can see, flames are still present on a number of floors and are shooting out of the roof. At one point, we are told, those flames were as high as a hundred feet over the top of the building. [*The photographer begins moving the shot downward toward an apartment.*] This is the third floor balcony from which a couple jumped trying to escape the flames. The two were killed in the fall. [*The photographer begins to pull out to a wider shot of firefighters pouring water on the flames.*] You can see dozens of firefighters here working to put out the fire ... and more are on their way. We are told that tens of thou-

sands of gallons of water have been used so far [*The
photographer shoots upward showing the fire and water
being blown around by the wind.*] but a lot of that water has gone to waste, and here you can see why. You
can see the water being blown all over the place by
the high winds here. I can even feel a light mist coming down on me as a result of the shift in the winds.
See the burning embers in the picture? They are becoming more of a concern because fire officials fear
they might ignite other fires in or on adjacent buildings. [*At this point, the photographer begins to focus in
on the other buildings.*] That is why, as you can see,
firefighters are spraying the rooftops and sides of
these buildings. Officials say the goal is to keep them
cool and wet. That way embers are less likely to cause
problems if they land on the structures. [*At this point
the photographer begins to pull the shot back and refo-
cus on the reporter, who will wrap up her report live on
camera.*] A third fire company has been called in to
assist in fighting the fire. The Salvation Army is here
to help those displaced by the fire. The mayor says he
is opening up two community centers that will be
used as temporary shelters to aid those left homeless
by the blaze. Reporting from the scene, I'm Amanda
Houston, back to you in the studio.

The anchor and reporter may then engage in a period of
question and answer for as long as necessary. This is a much
different form of live news. It is almost always reserved for
breaking news events where there is no time for anything
else. This presentation works well when the reporter is confident and has constructed a logical flow of the information

and live images. It requires the photographer and reporter to be telling the same story and watching and listening to each other as they are doing so. When done well, this format can be the most exciting for the reporter and photographer and conveys the newness or breaking nature of the story. When done wrong, it can make the reporter, crew, and news operation look panicked and unprofessional.

The Live Interview Shot

Finally, your live presentation may either include or center around a live interview. A *live interview* can help provide viewers with the most up-to-date information available. It may also help convey the emotion of a certain situation better than any words you could craft. The live interview subject might be an official updating the status of the fire. It might be a fire victim talking in detail about how he or she escaped the flames and what it will take to pick up the pieces of the life left charred in the remains of the apartment building. It might be a witness who either saw the fire begin or came on the scene and began helping to guide people out of the building. Many of the best hero stories can be found here.

The live interview may precede or follow a wraparound, a vo-sot, a vo, or a scene scan, or it may stand alone, depending on time and relevance. The goal is to use the interview as another element to enhance your coverage of the event—not repeat it. If you have an interview with the fire chief in your pretaped report, you probably do not need him live as well (unless circumstances have changed dramatically since you conducted the last interview). The same is true in the case of a live vo-sot. Interviewing the chief following your live vo is a nice way to set the scene and end by bringing us up to date with the interview at the end. The live interview can also be a great tool when no others are available. Here, the interview can augment or replace a majority of the scene scan taken when arriving on the scene just before air. Here is how the live interview at our fire scene might work best.

Anchor: Good evening ... two people are dead following a major fire on the city's northwest side. The blaze broke out around three thirty this afternoon at the Green View apartment complex. The fire is still not under control, and we understand that there are still some people trapped in their apartments. We go live now to Amanda Houston who is on the scene with the latest, Amanda?

Reporter: As you can see behind me, firefighters are using ladders to try and rescue a couple of residents trapped on their third floor apartment balcony. Fire officials tell us they are the last of the residents to be removed from the building. It has been a very difficult situation for much of the afternoon. High winds and low water pressure are wreaking havoc with firefighters who are trying to extinguish this blaze.

Here, the words "extinguish the blaze" become another cue. This time, they are a cue to the photographer to pull out a little wider on his shot to reveal the fire chief who has been standing next to the reporter for a couple of moments in advance of the live interview. The reporter then introduces and begins to interview the chief about the situation.

Reporter: I am joined now by Fire Chief Stan Waters for the latest on the situation. Chief, how much progress is being made at this point?

Fire Chief: Well, as you mentioned it has been a very difficult day for us so far. When we first arrived the fire was really out of control. Flames were shooting out of the top of the building and a number of the upper floor units were fully involved. It is still not completely under control, but we are making progress. The most important thing at this point is that everyone is accounted for and we are getting help.

Reporter: Chief, what can you tell us about the two victims of this fire?

Fire Chief: Unfortunately they panicked and did not wait for our rescue crews to pull them from the balcony. They jumped trying to escape the situation. People were encouraging them to stay put and telling them that help was on the way and would be there shortly. Unfortunately, in situations like this sometimes people just don't think clearly. Their instinct is to do whatever they can to get away from the smoke and flames, not recognizing that sometimes their actions can be as deadly as what they are dealing with at the time.

Reporter: What types of obstacles are your firefighters running into at this point in battling this blaze?

Fire Chief: The biggest concern right now is getting enough water on the fire. The winds are blowing very strong and gusting even stronger. Much of the water we are trying to spray on the fire is actually getting blown away from the flames. The key is to increase the number of working lines we have and hope for a shift in the winds.

Reporter: I see a number of firefighters hosing down the adjacent buildings; you are obviously concerned about the possibility that this fire will spread?

Fire Chief: You are exactly right. In this case we are dealing with a lot of fire in the primary building. We are also confronted with large burning embers flying around the scene. A number of those embers have already landed on other buildings and rooftops. Even a small ember is capable of touching off another big blaze. We keep water on the other structures to reduce the chance of ignition should an ember land on either the roof or siding.

Reporter: Chief, you have a number of firefighters already here, and I heard on the scanner that you called another alarm.

Fire Chief: That's right. At this point we are in need of more equipment and more bodies to get this thing under control. Some of our guys really need a rest. Many are just coming off of extensive training work, and others helped battle a tire fire in another county for several days, so it would be nice to get our numbers up and get some fresh bodies in here. You also have to remember that fighting fires in cold temperatures really takes its toll.

Reporter: Chief, thank you very much for bringing us up to date on the latest—we'll check in with you again soon.

Fire Chief: Thank you. Oh, be sure to tell people to stay away from this area for a while. It is going to be quite a mess!

At this point, the photographer is pulling out of the two shot with the reporter and chief, and focusing back on the reporter. The reporter then will take a few seconds to comment and add some closing thoughts or to recap the most important information covered during the interview.

Reporter: To recap, firefighters are making some progress on this spectacular fire at the Green View apartment complex. Two have been killed, but the fire chief says everyone else has been accounted for. Firefighters are still battling winds, and more help is on the way. We will keep you updated with any changes from the scene as they happen. For now, reporting live, I'm Amanda Houston, back to you in the studio.

The reporter and fire chief have done a pretty good job covering the nuts and bolts of the situation. It is unlikely that any question and answer between the reporter and anchor will be necessary at this point. However, this is a time-sensitive business. There may be a need to fill even more time or return to the reporter later in the newscast if there are any significant changes in the story.

We have discussed the majority of forms live television news reports will take and under what circumstances each is best used. It is important to note that no matter what form is used, the reporter can convey essentially the same information. You may not have the luxury of time or of resources, but that is not an excuse to give the viewer any less in terms of effort or perspective.

When you know what time constraints you are under and what you have to work with, it becomes much easier to craft your story and focus your attention on the task at hand. Arriving on a hectic fire scene can be difficult and sometimes even dangerous. A good live reporter will have a good sense of what he or she can accomplish given the circumstances and deadlines. There is no panic when you are focused on your goal and have a realistic picture of how much you can do. If you are focused, your live shot will be sharper and stronger no matter what form it takes.

2

The Presentation

There are few things in life that bring one as much excitement and satisfaction as pulling off a flawless live television news presentation. It is the ultimate test of the ability to combine skills and senses with poise and professionalism. This is a unique combination which yields an informative and polished presentation and builds credibility and confidence.

There are many reporters who are able to deliver stellar live presentations night in and night out. Unfortunately, there are many more who are inconsistent at best, or consistently inferior at worst. We have all seen very good live reporters and admired the work they do and the level of success they have achieved. Likewise, we have all witnessed terrible live reports and seen reporters who are struggling every step of the way. In many cases the difference between the consistently good live reporters and the consistently bad ones has less to do with talent and more to do with focus.

Models of Success

In live television news reporting, as in other fields, there are those that perform better than others under pressure. These individuals always stand out and generally set the standards by which others in the field will be judged. Let us look at some examples of success in other fields and how some of the principles for success in those fields apply to live television news reporting.

The Running Back: Moving Forward

The first model we will look at is the running back. In the national football league, every team has at least two running backs. Most are good at what they do, but only a handful ever reach hall of fame levels. What separates the best from the rest? In many cases it is talent, in others, sheer drive and determination. Focus and persistence are also among the attributes of the best running backs. When a hall of fame–caliber running back is handed the football, there is virtually no stopping him. He will run through holes created by his offensive line. When he is hit by a defender, he will continue to drive forward and push toward the end zone. Hall of fame–caliber backs know that one of the real keys to success is to keep the legs moving forward at all times.

In live television news reporting, moving forward at all times is also crucial. Here, of course, we are not talking about the legs, but about the mind and the mouth. Young reporters tend to fall or stumble when they "get hit" because they fail to keep the mind and mouth moving forward. Stumbles can be caused by a number of factors. A reporter may forget a word, mispronounce a word, or become distracted by something in the environment. Once the stumble occurs, the reporter is tripped up and generally stumbles again and again. The key here is to realize that one blown word is not the end of the world, nor should it mark the end of your live presentation.

There are few things more uncomfortable than tripping up on live television. A mistake often sends the reporter into a panic. This panic may cause the reporter to stop and apologize for the error, or to speed up his or her delivery. There is a common misconception among young and inexperienced reporters that they must not stop talking for even a millisecond until the camera is off of them. The reality is that a brief pause may be all that is needed to get back on track. The key to recovering from a stumble is knowing your material, knowing where you are going, and moving forward with your story.

The ability to recover from a mistake is tied to the structure of the story and the writing. If a story is well written and flows logically, the reporter will be able to move from thought A to thought C after stumbling over thought B. If, however, the story lacks flow and structure, the reporter is more likely than not to become lost and pick up the story at a point that makes little sense. Let's take a look at an example:

> **Anchor:** Three people are dead following a violent collision between a car and a minivan on the Kennedy expressway. The accident occurred around three this afternoon on the city's north side. Reporter Amanda Houston is live at the accident scene and joins us now with the details. Amanda?

Reporter: Police tell us that the minivan was traveling northbound at a high rate of speed when the driver apparently lost control of the vehicle. The van then crossed over the centerline and slammed into the car. The driver of the minivan and his passenger were killed on impact. The driver of the car died a short time later at a nearby hospital.

The reporter has structured the story in an easy to follow chronological order. Part A is all of the information preceding the crash. Part B is the impact point. Part C is the end result of it all. This is extremely helpful to the reporter in the event he or she stumbles over a word or is distracted by something. The reporter can move forward from the point of the mistake very easily because the events are being described in a certain order. The reporter is aware of where the story began and where it will end. Therefore, at the point of a mistake, the reporter can quickly assess where he or she must pick the story up and continue forward.

The Gymnast: Good Landings

There are any number of factors that can throw a reporter off stride and ruin a live shot. Some of these are out of the reporter's control, most though are not. You may notice that many reporters tend to stumble or get tongue-tied at the end of their live shots. In many cases this is because the reporter has spent too much time focused on the live introduction and body of the story while treating the wrap-up, or end of the piece, as an afterthought. It is important to realize that the end of your story is as important as any other part of it. It is also the last impression you leave with the viewer. It is similar in significance to the landing in gymnastics.

When an Olympic gymnast is preparing for a balance beam routine, she is sharply focused on the three major portions of the exercise on which she will be judged: the mount, the beam routine, and the dismount. In the mount, the gymnast skillfully and gracefully makes her way onto the beam. In the beam routine, the gymnast shows her skill in negotiating the narrow beam and her courage in movements above and atop the apparatus. Then the gymnast wraps up the routine with the dismount. Here the gymnast is focused on leaving the beam in a dramatic fashion and sticking the landing. To stick the landing, the gymnast must cleanly touch down with both feet without slipping, falling, or twisting. A bad landing can ruin an otherwise exceptional beam routine and cost the gymnast enough points to be eliminated from competition.

A live television news reporter can look at his or her presentation in a fashion similar to that of the gymnast's routine. The reporter's *mount* is of course the live introduction to the story being presented. The *routine* is the piece the reporter is introducing. This piece may be a prepackaged report, or package. It may also be the video (vo) and/or the sound on tape (sot) from an interview subject, or the live interview. The dismount is of course the reporter's live on-camera wrap-up. The quality of the reporter's live performance is judged on the execution of each element. A great live shot contains a strong introduction, a strong piece, and a strong wrap-up. Countless great introductions have been overshadowed by bad wrap-ups. In almost all of these cases, the reporter's lack of focus is to blame.

Basketball Superstars: Finding the Zone

The best live television news reporters are those that are the most focused when the camera is on. In fact, those at the top of just about any game are there because they have talent and focus. If you are to succeed in live television news, you need to learn to achieve a very high level of focus, known as the *zone*. You have no doubt witnessed or experienced this level of focus at some point in your life. One of the best examples of zone focus can be found in the performance of superstar basketball players. When these special players are in the zone, they are unstoppable. Every shot seems to fall, every obstacle is cleared in a seemingly effortless fashion. The zone is a state of mind whereby nothing at all can get in your way. The focus is so sharp that nothing can come between you and your objective.

When you are operating in the zone, the task at hand is all that matters, and everything else gets blocked out. As a live television news reporter you will be placed in situations that are at best chaotic and at worst next to impossible to contend with. Excelling at live television means overcoming all obstacles and moving ahead. There is no shortage of distractions in each and every live situation. Each of these distractions has the potential to throw you out of focus and into a live tailspin. Identifying and avoiding or defusing these distracting "mines" is your responsibility. Here is an example of a chaotic situation. See how many mines you can identify.

> **Scene:** It is an extremely hot and unbelievably humid afternoon. You arrive on the scene of a shooting. Several people have been shot, and at least one person is dead at the scene. Nearly a dozen police offi-

cers from the city and county are on the scene. Sirens are wailing as additional officers and ambulance personnel make their way to the location. There are dozens of people in the immediate area. Some are relatives of the shooting victims, others are friends. There are a number of others who came to the location after hearing the shots fired. The friends and relatives of the victims are emotionally distraught. There are screaming and crying coming from everywhere. A fight breaks out among several of the onlookers. Police become involved in the scuffle. Someone has set fire to a nearby dumpster filled with garbage. It smells terrible, and smoke from the fire is blowing back toward the center of the chaos. In the distance there is the sound of gunfire or fireworks—it is hard to tell the difference sometimes. A few members of the crowd turn their attention to you and your crew members. They are not pleased that you are there and begin shouting at you to leave. You are in the middle of it all and are less than two minutes away from a live update. Your producer is giving you instructions through your ear piece in one ear, and your photographer is talking in your other ear.

Had enough? There is more than enough to deal with in this scene, it is almost to the point of sensory overload. Mines are everywhere: The environment is hot and hostile. The noise is loud and all around you. The smoke is irritating to your eyes and throat. The stench in the air makes you feel sick to your stomach. And most of those at the scene would rather you were not there and have let you know that in no uncertain terms. Any one of these factors alone is enough to interfere with your presentation. When you add it all up, it becomes very easy to imagine the level of focus you will need to function effectively under this kind of stress.

In situations where there is little time and a lot to contend with, it becomes critical that the reporter reach the zone. Most reporters, however, do not. That is why you see some reporters struggle and stumble when reporting live under intense and adverse conditions. The successful live reporter is able to absorb all that is going on in the environment and block out the distractions long enough to complete his or her presentation. Admittedly, much of this ability comes with time, practice, and failure. The key is finding a way to properly prepare yourself for the live shot and making sure that prior to and during the presentation you are one hundred percent focused.

Tips for Finding Focus

In this business, you are judged every day on that few minutes you appear on camera. It may take an entire eight-hour day to prepare your story for a live shot, but in the end your success or failure hangs on how well you perform in that two- or three-minute window. Your day may have been a very stressful one and your environment may be filled with mines, but come news time, your head must be clear and you must be focused. Each successful live television news reporter has his or her own way of preparing for a live shot. There is no right or wrong method for getting focused. The rule is, if it works for you, it works. Below are some general tips you may want to consider as you search for your own approach.

The Five-Minute Rule

You are free to complain about or agonize over anything and everything until five minutes before your live shot. Feel free to get it all out of your system. If it is a Murphy's law day, where anything that can go wrong has gone wrong, talk it over with your photographer. If your hair is a mess and the weather is not to your liking, whine about it for a while. Take issue with anything you can find fault in and talk it out before that five-minute mark. Once you have hit the five-minute mark, the only thing that should be on your mind is the live shot. At this point, you must be reading the script you are about to deliver or rehearsing the live portion of your report that is not scripted. You must not allow anything to interfere with your preparation for the live shot once that five-minute mark is reached.

Focus on the Lens

One of the best ways to get focused is by focusing in on the lens that will be focusing on you. Since you will be looking at the camera lens when you begin your live report, it is a natural place to focus your attention prior to the live shot. Many reporters stare deeply into the lens as they rehearse for their live shots. It is important to find a focal point, like the camera lens, if you are to be focused. When you concentrate on something and review your presentation over and over, you find that all of the things that could distract you do not.

Stretching Exercises

Many reporters like to stretch out before a live shot. Simple stretching exercises can help reduce anxiety, loosen you up so you don't appear stiff when on air, and, if it is exceptionally cold, warm you up. Stretching can also help reduce the levels of nervous energy in your system prior to a live shot and improve your focus. Some of the most common stretching exercises involve the neck, shoulder, back, and legs. Most of these exercises can be done without leaving the spot you will be in for your live presentation.

Neck: There are two commonly used exercises to loosen the neck: the neck roll and the chin drop. The neck roll involves tilting your head back then rolling it to the right side, back to center, then to the left side. The second is the chin drop. The chin drop involves tilting your head all the way back. The head is then slowly raised to the standard position. Finally, the chin is dropped forward to the chest.

Shoulder: The most common shoulder exercise is the shoulder shrug. Standing in place, simply move your shoulders upward, hold to a count of five, then return them to their normal resting spot.

Back: Most standing exercises involving the back are of the leaning and twisting nature. Stand with your hands on your hips, feet firmly planted, and rotate your torso to the left. Hold that position for a five count then return to normal. Repeat the same only this time turn to your right side.

Legs: There are a variety of standing exercises designed to stretch the legs. The most common are toe-touches, which work on the back of the legs, or lean-ins. Lean ins involve placing one leg in front of the other in a sprinter's stance then leaning forward on the leg that is out in front. Reverse the stance then lean forward on the other leg.

Obviously your goal is not to undertake a complete workout here. The purpose is to find techniques that will help you relax. The more relaxed you are, the better you will feel going into the live shot. Many reporters find that a few stretches go a long way toward loosening them up for the presentation.

Special Concerns

Failure by Letdown

While it can be difficult to *become* focused in surroundings that are chaotic, it is often easy to *lose* focus in situations where the story or surroundings provide little sensory stimulation. Take the following case for example:

Scene: Your live shot is scheduled to lead off the ten o'clock news cast. It is eight o'clock. Your story is on a local council meeting where a vote was taken to approve the city budget. There is little in terms of excitement or controversy here to keep you on the edge. In fact, you have already covered a number of the chief budget items in other stories in the past few weeks. Your story is completed well before the newscast. You are already tired. (Some of those council meetings can really take it out of you!) You have rehearsed your script for over an hour and are confident in your delivery. The location for the live shot is outside of city hall on a Monday evening. It is as quiet as can be. Your photographer is playing cards with the live truck operator at this point. In short, you are all very bored waiting for the newscast.

This is not the type of story that provides much in terms of excitement, nor do the surroundings challenge your senses. There are no apparent mines. This is when things are really dangerous. The problem with this scene is that the reporter will often fail to focus enough on the presentation and will blow the live shot due to a lack of attention. It is known as failure by letdown. It is similar in many respects to the way players and teams prepare themselves for not so exciting opponents. The best team in the league may be going up against the worst. The mental preparation on the part of the best team may be lacking. They are more talented and are expected to win. The trouble is that there are no "gimmies" in either sports or live shots. The end result of a lack of focus is almost always failure.

This is another case where the ritual of getting into your zone five minutes before air is critical. Doing so forces you to concentrate as hard on the so called "lame" live shots as on the exciting breaking news live presentations. Clearing your mind of everything, including boredom in this case, will give you the edge you need to maintain consistency.

Another thing to keep in mind is that these lame lives are just as important as any other live shot you will ever do. This becomes clear when you are job hunting. You are not likely to include the city hall live shot on your resume tape. The resume tape contains your best work. It is the tape you send out to news directors hoping to wow them with your best stuff. If you are successful in getting his or her attention, the news director will likely ask you for another tape. This time he or she will want a tape of the stories you have done in the past week, including the city hall piece. If you blew that shot because you took it too lightly, you may have also blown the job opportunity. Some advice on the matter from Chicago news anchor and reporter Melissa Ross:

> You have to approach every live shot as if it is going to appear on your resume tape. If you are new to this, just pretend that this is the only live shot you are going to get to do, the only one you will get to send to news directors, so it has to be perfect. As a reporter with a little bit or a lot of experience, these shots are also important. I received a call not long ago from a news director. He is a man who has called me two or three times in my career. He called my agent and said, "I like her tape, send me everything she has done in the last week." [News directors] do this routinely because they want to see everything you have done recently. If it is not as perfect as what you have on your resume tape, they assume sometimes that you are not consistent, and therefore are not what they are looking for. It may not be true, but as we know, perception is reality. Approach everything as if it is going onto a resume tape.

The Weather

There are times when mother nature poses the most difficulty in terms of maintaining focus and getting your story across cleanly. No matter where you are, weather will always produce stories and hamper the ability to cover stories. Weather can have a dramatic impact on your live presentation. Some areas of the country deal with weather-related stories much more than others. In areas where there are dramatic seasonal differences in temperature and precipitation, covering the weather is a year-round event. Let's look at just some of the stories you can always count on.

Spring: The spring brings with it a host of weather-related offerings. Flooding is almost always a problem this time of year. In the South and Midwest, tornadoes and severe thunderstorms are among the top stories of the season.

Summer: The heat and humidity are responsible for many of the stories you will cover. Heat kills. In Chicago's infamous 1995 heat wave, more than seven hundred people died from heat related illness. Heat combined with a lack of rainfall means drought. Each year hundreds of thousand of dollars worth of crops either burn up in the fields or never get out of the ground.

Fall: Rain and some tornadic activity are again a concern. Tropical storms and hurricanes tend to be most destructive. These types of storms can have a devastating impact on people and property.

Winter: Extreme cold weather kills people, cars, and anything else that spends too much time in it. This time of year people die trying to stay warm, as when space heaters burn down homes. In addition, snow and ice shut down highways and runways, stranding travelers everywhere.

How a reporter looks and acts when presenting weather-related news can have a significant impact on credibility. Consider the following scene:

Six inches of snow have fallen in and around the city over a very short period of time. The snow is covering ice that had already formed on many of the main streets and certainly on most of the residential roads in the area. The actual air temperature is in the single digit range, the windchill brings things to well below zero. There are literally hundreds of accidents citywide. Some are minor fender benders; others are major accidents involving injuries. The heavy snow is weighing down power lines, and many have snapped, cutting power to thousands of people. Repair crews are having a hard time reaching problem areas. Road crews are out in force trying to clear streets, but it is slow going here as well. A ground stop has been called at the local airport, which means all outbound flights are staying put. A health advisory has been issued. City officials and medical experts are advising people to stay off of the streets and stay inside if at all possible. The windchills are at a dangerous level, at the point where exposed skin can freeze within less than two minutes. Homeless shelters are packed to capacity. Making matters worse, the snow is not expected to let up anytime soon and another bad weather system appears to be right behind this one.

The first obstacle this scene presents to you as a live reporter is getting to work! If you are able to do that, there are a host of other hurdles you must clear to be able to piece together an informative report that contains essential information and looks credible as well. Usually, in news stories which contain this many elements, you will be called upon to bring together several highlights for your live presentation. For example, your assignment is to gather information, video, and sound on the transportation side of the weather emergency. You are responsible for finding car accidents or vehicles in the ditch. You will also need shots of snow plows and interviews with a plow driver. In addition, there are passengers who are stranded at the airport, and you will need to talk with some of them. Train and bus traffic is also slowed to a crawl, at best. You are expected to bring these elements together and present them live at six o'clock.

Your live shot will be from a rest area overlooking the main interstate leading into and out of the city. This brings up the second obstacle in this scene: it is no easier for a television news crew to navigate snow-covered and ice-slicked streets than it is for anyone else. You are working the story and working in the story as well. This can add stress to deadline pressures.

In the best-case scenario, you have been able to find everything you set out to find. Now you are at the overpass preparing your live report. The weather conditions extended your travel time considerably, thus reducing your story preparation time substantially. You are writing and reviewing tape. The live truck heater is not working all that well. You are giving no thought at all to the things you forgot to bring with you. After all, this storm caught everyone off guard, including you. Your warm scarf is at home, your nice hat is in your car. The gloves you have are the ones you grabbed as you were running out the door, not the warm ones you would have selected if you had been prepared for the storm. You are wearing a warm coat, but not your warmest winter coat, the one you put away for the season, not expecting another Arctic blast. You will be thinking about all of this soon enough.

Fortunately you have some extra time before your live presentation. You don't necessarily want to leave the relative warmth of the live truck to assume your position for the shot, but you have to so lighting can be adjusted and other technical portions of the shot can be checked. It is here, standing in front of the camera lens with the bitter winds blowing through you and the snow flying into your face that you begin to realize that you are not really prepared for all of this. Still, you work to focus your attention on what you will be saying and focus less on how cold you are.

By the time your live shot hits, you are beyond cold; you feel frozen, and you have only been standing there for a couple of minutes. But, as your report so correctly points out, that is all it takes to freeze that unexposed skin. Remember, you forgot that hat and scarf!

Cold weather and wind can have a dramatic impact on your delivery. Bone-chilling windchills can slow your jaw action, which makes it very difficult to talk at a regular pace. Bitter temperatures also tend to make people tense their muscles, making them look and feel stiff. In addition, cold can make it difficult to maintain consistent eye contact. Many people naturally squint or blink frequently in conditions like this. In spite of all of this you are able to find your focus and deliver your presentation clearly. Your report certainly sounded credible to the average viewer. The trouble here is that the report didn't look credible.

You never want to be in a situation where your own actions are being viewed by the audience as contradictory to your message. You were correct to inform viewers that uncovered skin freezes quickly in a couple of minutes or less. The viewer, however, is left wondering why, if it is so dangerous, you are not wearing a scarf around your exposed neck and your ears not covered with either muffs or hat flaps. You were correct to report that the majority of body heat is lost through the top of the head, but the viewer then wonders why you are not wearing a hat. Viewers understand that you are out in the elements for a reason. They are aware of the fact that you have a job to do. However, it is only natural to call into question what you are saying and what is being advised by experts in your report when you are not heeding the same advice.

In other cases, your look doesn't necessarily detract from the credibility of your story; instead it distracts the viewer from your piece. If you are reporting on a heat wave and the drought it is causing, a withering cornfield makes a good back drop. If you are wearing a suit and tie while talking about the intense heat and all of the problems it is causing, the viewer will likely begin questioning your choice in clothing instead of listening to much of what you are saying. It sounds basic and rather obvious, but time and time again, experienced and inexperienced reporters undermine otherwise good live reports simply by their choices in clothing.

A way to avoid these problems is simply to be prepared. Many news reporters have "go bags" at their desks or in their cars. These bags contain appropriate clothing for a variety of situations: clothing you might want to change into quickly in the event you must cover a flood, for example.

Boots, extra socks, pants, a more casual shirt, a sweater, hats, and a pair of comfortable walking shoes or gym shoes are some of the things you might want to keep in your go bag. Remember to add and subtract items from the bag as seasons begin to change.

Delivery

One area of focus that often gets overlooked in the process of preparation for live television is delivery. Many reporters rehearse their scripts and talk out what they are planning to say over and over again. Unfortunately, time deadlines and environmental factors often keep the reporter from really practicing the delivery. Every reporter will develop his or her own style in terms of presenting a story. Some are more vocally dramatic than others. Many have unique approaches to the mechanics of storytelling. What all good live reporters have in common though is the ability to tell a story clearly and cleanly. There are three factors that contribute to a good delivery no matter what the voice or style: pronunciation, enunciation, and tone.

Pronunciation

Pronunciation is the placing of stress and intonation on syllables, words, and phrases. Pronunciation mistakes are among the easiest for viewers to catch. It is important to make sure that you know not only what you are saying in your report, but also how to say it. Hard to pronounce names or words should be broken down into syllables and written out phonetically. Phonetic spellings are basically the translation of words as they sound, not necessarily as they are spelled. Some mispronounced words are very common.

Milk is a good example. In some cases, milk is pronounced (mel-k). The stress is on the "l" rather than the "i.". In Egypt, there is a city named Cairo, pronounced (ki-ro). In Illinois, there is a city named Cairo, pronounced (ka-ro). If you are unsure of the correct pronunciation of a word, consult the dictionary or find another word. If you are uncertain of how to correctly pronounce a person's name, be sure to ask. Many people are very excited to appear on television for the first, and maybe only, time in their lives. These people have been good enough to help you with an interview for your report. The least you can do is pronounce their names properly. If you are uncertain of the pronunciation of a city or town, ask the locals.

Enunciation

Enunciation is to clearly and distinctly pronounce words. This can be one of the easiest areas in which to make a mistake when in the throes of a live presentation. You must be very clear if you expect the viewer to understand what you are saying. Slurring words together can throw you and the viewer off. Take great care to separate each word from the others as you move through a sentence. This is especially important when you are using words with the same first letter. Keeping words separate can be difficult at times, especially in the case of breaking news, where nothing is prescripted. The best way to train yourself is to use common-letter sentence lines. One of the most common of these tongue twisters is a variation of "Sister Sally sells seashells by the seashore." There are a number of speech workbooks available that can provide you with plenty of practice material. You can also craft your own practice sentences and work through them regularly.

Tone

The days of the big booming bass voice in broadcasting are gone. That is not to say that these voices don't exist; they are just not a requirement for employment in live television newscasting. These days, people want reporters to talk to them. Viewers don't want a story yelled at them. Most certainly don't appreciate having a live television news reporter vocally ramming the story down their throats. The key is a conversational tone.

Reporters tend to forget sometimes that they are communicating to individual people. The tendency is to view the audience in mass. It is important to learn how to communicate to everyone by talking to one person. There are many ways to accomplish this. Deliver your report as you would to a friend or family member. Picture one individual to represent the audience. In radio, this is easily accomplished by placing a photograph of that person on a copy stand. In television, you have to keep that picture in your mind. Avoid being stiff and stern in your delivery; both faults are easily identified by viewers. Avoid faking a voice. We have all heard those disc jockey voices that are forced and contrived for reasons that most of us still don't understand. If you don't sound real, you don't look real. Remember, good habits adopted early in your career help build it—bad ones help end it.

Body Language and Props

Many reporters believe that it is the mind and the mouth that tell the story. The truth of the matter is that most successful live television news reporters have mastered the ability to use their entire body to tell the story.

What really boosts a presentation is movement. A stiff

and awkward reporter looks stiff and awkward. A conversational reporter naturally uses his or her face and hands to help tell a story. Think about some of the more animated conversations you have had with family or friends. These usually involve some facial expressions and some gesturing. This is exactly what you are looking for in your live presentation. It is only natural to have some animation when you are telling a story. The nature of the story will dictate how much and what kind.

Facial expressions can add humor to funny feature reports. A somber facial tone can help support the nature of a tragic live report. You should never fake emotion for the sake of expression. At the same time, you should never avoid showing expressions that come naturally. You are human. Props are also not a bad idea if you have them and they fit the story. If your live report is about a five-hundred-page indictment of a politician, don't be afraid to hold up the text and show it to viewers. You are telling a story. Relax; be true to yourself and your audience. You will find that live television news is much more comfortable, much more fun, and much more real when you allow yourself to be all of these things.

3

Notes—No Notes

There is an axiom in this business, live by the notes—die by the notes. When and how to use notes in your live presentation is a very important consideration. You have no doubt seen live reports where the reporter is reading from his or her notepad and looking up occasionally into the camera lens. In other cases, reporters begin with a memorized line or two then glance down at the notepad and begin reading their script. Yet there are others who have a notepad in their hands but never seem to look at it during the presentation. As live television news reporters, we all take and use notes, but how we use them impacts how we look on the air. How to use notes is one of the key concepts in both the teaching and the learning of live television presentation.

Reading the Notes: Overreliance

Nerves

Few things look as awkward on television as a reporter who is constantly looking down and reading a story to the audience right off of the notepad. When reporters look down at notepads too often or at times when they shouldn't, they are "diving for copy." This happens when the reporter lacks the confidence to pull away from the script and talk the story. This usually occurs in the early years of live presentation development, when the tendency is to stick to the written word. This is especially true in a classroom environment, as Northwestern University professor Patricia Dean explains.

> Quite often most of the students are very nervous and want to write it all out and read it all as they have written [it]. It takes me a while to tell them to throw the paper away because they are really looking nervous. Some people are good at memorizing and can talk it through. This is very effective. But for someone that is nervous, when you mis-speak words you are setting yourself up for other problems. Someone who is nervous tends to be weak under stress. What I suggest to them is to not memorize. I encourage them to remember key points and talk them through. If you have notes, just have the key points of the story jotted down. Occasionally, though, when I have someone who has a difficult time with confidence, I tell them to throw the paper down and tell me the story. I work with very bright young people. They do remember the key facts of a story and they really do know their stories. It just takes them a while to get comfortable with telling them. What I stress is that the journalism is the toughest part. I had one student in my class who tried to memorize everything and had notes in front of her. She was very nervous. So I said to her, let's put the notes aside and try this once. She did it and was markedly better. Eventually, she learned to keep her notes down in front of her so she could glance down if needed.

Notes as a Crutch

Notes should be used to help a reporter present the story, but they should not become a crutch. There can be real trouble if a reporter comes to rely on notes too much. For example, if a reporter scripts his or her live report word for word and something happens to the scripted story, the report is doomed. What could happen to the script? High winds have been known to blow a page or two of a report away. Reporters have also been known to drop notepads or pages of prepared script before or during the live report. Even if nothing happens to the script, reading word for word is not the ideal way to present a story. This is because in most cases it sounds like you are reading a story to the viewer, not telling one.

The prepared script is a safety net for many young reporters. This is okay early on. Learning to deliver a report and building confidence in the presentation is very important. Over time, the reporter should learn to rely less on what he or she has written and more on knowledge of the material. The more you know about your story, the better you will be able to tell it to others.

Reducing the Need for Notes

Learn to Organize

The best live television news presenters are often the best news writers. There is a clear correlation between the ability to write well and the ability to talk a story. Good writers are able to bring forth the most important points of a story and present them in an easy to understand and logical fashion. The more organized the story, the easier it is to tell. Many reporters fail in their live presentations because their reports are disorganized, are not focused, lack direction, or simply contain too much information. These are often the same reporters who find it all but impossible to put down the notepad and tell the story.

There are any number of right ways to tell the same story. If you watch three reporters on the scene of the same event, they will all present the facts a little bit differently. As different as the reports may sound, they follow some basic and important structural rules. Organization is the key in all cases. If a report is not well organized, it will come across that way to the viewer. It is important to be able to present your information in a clear and concise manner. It is also important to present the most important information first and the less important information later. Let's look at an organized report and one that is not as well organized.

Anchor: Good evening. There is a major accident to report tonight on the city's busiest expressway. A number of cars and a truck are involved. We go live now to reporter Amanda Houston who is at the scene with the latest information. Amanda?

Reporter: Fire officials say five people are dead and at least a dozen more are being treated for serious injuries from this accident. Two other victims remain trapped inside their vehicle, and rescue workers are trying to treat them for injuries while at the same time working to remove them from the mangled wreckage. The accident occurred about twenty minutes ago. Witnesses tell us that a semitrailer traveling northbound went out of control and crossed over several lanes before smashing into a concrete divider. Several cars were unable to stop and slammed into the truck. One of those cars exploded on impact, killing the driver and passenger instantly. In all, a half dozen cars and a van were involved. There was some concern at first that the semi might have been hauling hazardous materials, but the fire department confirmed that the tank trailer was empty at the time of the accident. The truck driver escaped injury. Traffic is expected to be blocked here for hours as crews work to clear the wreckage. Reporting live from the scene, I'm Amanda Houston, back to you in the studio.

This story is clear and concise. It conveys the magnitude and the tragedy of the situation right off the top. It conveys the urgency of the rescue attempt and the breaking nature of the accident. It then goes on to explain what happened and what the aftermath means for the rest of the driving public. The story flows very well and is easy for the viewer to understand. Now let's look at the same facts presented in a different way.

Anchor: Good evening. There is a major accident to report tonight on the city's busiest expressway. A number of cars and a truck are involved. We go live now to reporter Amanda Houston who is at the scene with the latest information. Amanda?

Reporter: Traffic around here is quite a mess. It will take workers hours to clean up the accident scene here. The mishap occurred about twenty minutes ago. The accident involves a truck and a half dozen cars. The truck was not carrying hazardous material at the time of the accident, according to fire officials. The truck driver was not injured in the accident, but five people were killed. A dozen other people were hurt in the crash and are being treated. Witnesses say the semitrailer was traveling north when it went out of control. It crashed into a concrete divider after crossing over several lanes. Several cars hit the truck. One of those cars exploded when it hit the truck. The driver and passenger in that car died. There are still two people trapped in one of the cars. Rescue workers are treating them and trying to get them out now. Reporting live from the scene, I'm Amanda Houston, back to you in the studio.

This story contains all of the same facts as the first one. However, it is much more difficult to follow and lacks a logical flow. It sounds like the reporter is stringing together a bunch of facts, not weaving them together as a good reporter might. The first report is logically presented. In the event of a stumble or mistake, the reporter would likely be able to move on quickly to the next thought because the material is presented in an order that is simple to understand. In the second story, the reporter might be hard pressed to figure out how to get back on track since the report is disorganized and lacks any real direction to begin with.

Focus on Relevance

Simplify

Live news reporting is a business of boiling down the complex into the simple. In most cases, you will have just a couple of minutes to tell a very involved tale. Unfortunately, many reporters do not know how to process the information they have in the most effective manner. This leads to trouble in the live presentation. Many reporters will fill their notepads with facts and figures that they find interesting, but that really matter little when weighed against the other information and time constraints. In almost every story you do, you will have more information than you will ever be able to use. This is where the ability to recognize the most important facts is critical.

The traffic accident scene we just visited is filled with plenty of information that is relatively useless to you as a reporter: Three of the cars involved in the accident were the same color. Hubcaps from some of the cars came off during the accident. The posted speed limit is 55 miles per hour. The road is asphalt, not concrete. All of these are undisputed facts. But they are facts that do little to add to your report. We make mental and written notes of a lot of this type of information, but when it comes to preparing the story, most of it should be discarded.

If your report is not well structured and contains many facts that do little to help move it along, it will stall, and you will likely stumble at one point or another. When you do stumble, you will look down at your notepad for a logical point to pick up the story, only to focus on the fact that three of the cars are the same color.

Get to the Point

If you are a good writer, you have developed the discipline of getting to the point and focusing on the information that is relevant to the story. If you are only going to have a few minutes for your introduction, live report, and conclusion, you do not want to be going in three or four different directions. If you have good information, give it right off the top. If you have good video, write to it and get to it quickly. The same is true when you have good sound from witnesses or officials. A good writer cuts to the chase and is truly focused on what the story really is. If you have discipline when it comes to broadcast writing, it is going to show day in and day out—especially in your live reports. This is something some students catch on to quicker than others according to Patricia Dean.

> A technique that I use when teaching is having the students do a long live shot. In one class I had them do a forty-five-second live shot, which to them felt really short. The next week I told them to use the same forty-five seconds a different way. I told them to talk for about thirty seconds and then do a question and answer segment for fifteen seconds. I told them to do the same thing they had done before only this time, move the information. Move something into the question and cut down the talk. A couple of the students remarked to me that the shorter ones seemed better. I asked them why. They said having more time made them try to cram in too much information. The shorter ones made them really select what was key to know for it. The hope here and the lesson is that you learn to find the story within the story and learn how to better select the facts. This is still a medium where the audience has to understand

and learn the first time through. I teach this the way I teach writing. One fact per sentence and no more. There should be no wasted sentences. If you don't have any time to waste, as in a live setting, then don't give me a sentence that really says nothing. On the other hand, don't put so much information in that I can't follow. Break it up! What I have found is that when students understand this then look back at their live shots, they recognize what went wrong. They realize that things were too confusing. I had one young man say to me, "I put too much into it, but I thought it was all important." So I asked him if there was a better way to do it and got him working on that.

Use one thought per sentence and use sentences that flow well into one another. These techniques will strengthen your presentation and reduce the need for notes. Ideally, the notes you use for your live report should be minimal and should contain only the information that is really important to the story. Some of the best speakers use notes. They do not, however, read their entire speech verbatim from a script. Most use index cards or notepads listing key phrases or concepts to be covered in the speech, organized in the order in which they should be discussed. Your notes as a live reporter should follow the same rules.

Learn What to Memorize

It is a good idea to memorize the first few lines of your live report. Then you can rely on the highlighted notes you have written down to present the rest of the information. The goal is to avoid, as often as possible, being seen on camera reading your notes. This is easier in some cases, more difficult in others. The extent to which you reference your notes is also dependent on the form your live presentation takes.

In the case of a wraparound package live shot, where you are introducing a prepackaged report then tagging it out live, you should work toward operating without notes at all. In this case, try to memorize both the two or three lines leading into the piece and the tag. You may want to start by keeping your lead-in and tag short. As you build confidence, you can add a line or two. Remember, though, that there is no need to extend a lead-in just because you can and are comfortable doing so. You still need to keep in mind that short and strong is always better than weak and long. You must also remember your roll cue (the cue to the studio to play your prepackaged report). The roll cue is the last three words you say leading into the piece. If you forget or skip the roll cue, there will be a delay in rolling the tape. This does not look good, nor does it make the producer and director happy.

In the case of a live vo-sot, it is best to memorize the introduction as well. It is also good practice to remember one additional line, the first line into video. In the case of a live vo-sot, the reporter appears on camera for the introduction. Video is rolled when the reporter hits the first roll cue. The reporter continues with the narration as the viewer sees the video. When the reporter hits the second roll cue, the sound bite is then rolled. The reporter stops talking, and the viewer hears from the interview subject in the short pretaped bite. At the end of the sound, the reporter is back out, live on camera, to wrap up the story.

There are two ways to handle the scripting of this report. The reporter can either write down everything and read it or write down the key concepts and tell the story following a series of highlights or bullet points. In either case, the introduction should be committed to memory and not read off a notepad. The reporter should also memorize the first line after the roll cue. This would be a line normally delivered when the video is rolled and the reporter is not seen on camera. This line should be memorized because there is often a brief delay between the time the reporter hits the roll cue and the time the tape is actually rolled. Usually, the reporter will look down at his or her notes after hitting the roll cue. If the tape is not taken quickly enough, the viewer will see the reporter glance down and begin to read. This is not a terrible mistake, but it is also not the cleanest of live presentations. Memorizing that extra line will help keep things looking sharp in the event tape is not taken on time.

We will use the first of the two accident scripts from earlier in this chapter to illustrate this point.

Anchor: Good evening. There is a major accident to report tonight on the city's busiest expressway. A number of cars and a truck are involved. We go live now to reporter Amanda Houston who is at the scene with the latest information. AMANDA?

Reporter: Fire officials say five people are dead and at least a dozen more are being treated for serious injuries from this accident.

This is the first line of the story. "From this accident" is the roll cue to video, the point at which video from the scene will be played over the narration of the reporter. The reporter should memorize all or the majority of the second line in this case as well, just in case the video does not appear as quickly as it should.

> **Reporter:** Two other victims remain trapped inside their vehicle, and rescue workers are trying to treat them for injuries while at the same time working to remove them from the mangled wreckage.

Once the video is taken, the reporter refers either to a verbatim script or to the series of highlighted details. The choice is a matter of comfort. In general, the more comfortable the reporter is with the story, the less reliance there is on a predrafted script. However, it should be noted that there are many very talented live reporters who still prefer writing every word they will say down on paper.

There are a number of cases where writing such a script is important. If you are quoting someone, it is best written exactly as quoted. Paraphrasing and quoting are different, legally and otherwise. It is also a good idea to write down much of your script if there are exact figures used. Statistics and dollar amounts are best given precisely rather than rounded up or down by the reporter.

Use Talking Points (Outline)

Creating an outline for your live report is one of the best ways to get your thoughts in order. You will want to write down your lead. This you will commit to memory, but seeing it on paper may help you organize the rest of your thoughts. After the lead, list the important facts of the story you want to convey in the live shot. Write down a few words about each. These words will be the trigger points for remembering what needs to be explained. Do this for each point you wish to cover. Rank the items in order of importance. These will be your talking points. Remember, if you are not reading verbatim, you are talking the story. Talking the story is typically a better approach to storytelling. It is more natural. For the car accident on the expressway, the following may be your talking points. The lead line remains the same.

Reporter: Fire officials say five people are dead and at least a dozen more are being treated for serious injuries from this accident. [Now list the talking points:]

1. Two still trapped
2. Rescue workers treating
3. Occurred 20 minutes ago
4. Semi northbound—hit divider
5. 6 cars hit truck—1 explodes
6. No haz mat situation
7. Driver uninjured

[Then it is back live to the reporter for the tag, which is memorized.]

Reporter: Traffic is expected to be blocked here for hours as crews work to clear the wreckage. Reporting live from the scene, I'm Amanda Houston, back to you in the studio.

The talking points help guide you through the information and allow you to devote as much time as you need to each point. You can talk more about the two trapped in the car and maybe a little bit less about some of the other things farther down the list. If you stumble over a thought or forget where you are going with the story, all you need do is look at the next point on the list and begin talking about that.

This type of outline also helps keep notes condensed. If you are writing out everything, there is a good chance you will have to turn a page or two doing your presentation. This has risks. If you turn to the wrong page, there will be an awkward pause as you try to find the right one. You may lose a page. The sound of page turning is also often heard through the microphone. Remember, you are working to pull off the cleanest presentation possible.

You may also add a talking point or two that may not be used. These points would be used in cases where you are asked to fill more time or engage in a question and answer exchange with the studio anchor. You may want to put a check mark by these points to denote them as optional. This way you do not automatically move on to them as you do to other items on the list.

The key to becoming less dependent on notes is to be more than prepared for your live presentation. Know the story. Focus on your information. Concentrate on what you must say. Rehearse your live shot and then do it. A good tightrope walker can cross from point A to point B without falling into the safety net. A great tightrope walker can cross from point A to point B without a safety net.

Breaking News: Working without Notes

One of the main reasons you work to rely less on notes is to be prepared for breaking news stories. These stories come out of nowhere. These are the news events that challenge all of your abilities as a reporter. In most cases, reporters have time to write or outline a live presentation. In breaking news situations, however, the reporter is often live on the air just minutes after arriving on the scene.

Use Your Environment

Breaking news is clearly the most challenging form of live presentation. You must be the eyes and ears of the public when you have not seen or heard anything in advance: You have just arrived. You have little information and little time to prepare. The distractions are incredible, but you must be able to draw everything you have together to talk the story. You must see and hear everything around you while filtering out what is important and discarding what is not important. If you can pull off a clean and informative report under these circumstances, you will experience the rush that comes with good live television news reporting. How do you do this with the odds seemingly stacked against you, when you have nothing prepared and have little if any information? The answer is simple. You focus on what you do have, which is quite a lot.

Let's go back to our expressway accident again. This time you will be the reporter and will arrive on the scene just minutes before your live report. You are in a good location; that is, you have a pretty good perspective of what is going on and who is on scene. You only know that five people are dead and a dozen more are being treated for injuries. This will be your lead information. From there, you must use your eyes, mind, and mouth to tell us what is going on in a very chaotic setting.

The Scene: You are able to see that six cars and a semi are involved in the accident. One car is charred—obviously burned as a result of the impact. Paramedics are running IV lines into one car which is upside down, and rescue workers are attending to the victims trapped in the car. At the same time, workers outside the car are using the jaws of life and other tools to tear open the vehicle in an attempt to free the victims. You can tell what direction the vehicles were traveling in prior to the impact. It is clear that the semi crossed over a number of lanes before making impact and coming to rest. You see a number of ambulances on scene. A vehicle from the coroner's office is also there. Tow trucks have arrived, and crews from the department of transportation are awaiting clearance from police and rescue personnel before attempting a cleanup. You notice a state trooper near the cab of the truck involved in the accident. A man with him climbs in and retrieves a book. He hands it to the officer. The logo on the man's hat matches the logo on the tank trailer. This is the driver of the truck handing over his log book and other papers to the officer. It is pretty clear to you that the driver has suffered no major injuries as he is up walking around and talking with authorities. And all you need do is look behind you to see the traffic backup, which is now about two miles long and growing by the minute.

Without writing down or scripting anything, you have all the elements of a live report right before your eyes. Now the key is to mentally organize them and work to present them in as clear and logical a fashion as possible. Begin by giving us an overview of the scene. Who is there? What are they doing? Find focal points that you and your photojournalist can zoom in on. This is helpful for a couple of reasons. First, it centers attention on an important aspect of the story, such as the entrapment. Second, it takes you off camera. It is sometimes easier to talk the story when you are focused on describing what you are seeing. This also gives you a chance to look around off camera and decide where you want to take the story next.

Watch for Changes

Watch for changes at the scene. You may see additional manpower or equipment being brought in to help. This is the latest information. Look for things that humanize the accident.

> **The Scene:** There are groups of people gathered near the site. Some are bandaged up; others are in tears. Some are victims treated at the scene while others are onlookers drawn to the scene out of curiosity. Out of the corner of your eye you notice a helicopter approaching the scene. It is not a news or traffic chopper; it is an emergency transport chopper. This clearly indicates that a victim in critical condition is about to be airlifted to a nearby trauma center for treatment.

Your instant scene scanning live report might sound something like this:

> **Reporter:** Fire officials say five people are dead and at least a dozen more are being treated for seri-

ous injuries from this accident. As you can see [*the camera pans away from you to the focal point*], rescue workers are trying to free two people who remain trapped in their overturned car. There are also a couple of paramedics leaning in the window and treating the victims in the car. I can see one paramedic starting an IV line and another pulling bandaging material from an emergency kit. It looks as if workers on the outside are making progress: a good portion of the rear roof of the vehicle has been sawed away and two doors have been removed. As we look to the right, you can see the varying degrees of damage to the cars involved. All of the vehicles struck the semi. The truck and cars were all northbound. Clearly, the truck crossed at least three lanes before hitting the concrete wall. Several of the cars that hit the truck are severely damaged. You can see that one of the cars appears to have exploded or caught fire on impact. There is little left of the vehicle, just charred remains. I count a half a dozen cars in all. You can see a police officer and another man at the cab of the truck. The logo on the man's hat matches the logo on the tank trailer. He is retrieving a book and paper from the driver's side of the cab. It would appear that this is the truck driver handing over his log book and other information to the officer. And as you might imagine, traffic on this stretch of expressway is at a dead halt and will be for quite some time.

This would be a pretty good live shot for a reporter just arriving on the scene. You are telling us what you can, what you know and avoiding those things you don't know. You are not speculating about things for which you have no information. You are telling us what is happening in real time. You are giving a big picture perspective while focusing in on specific important details of the accident.

Yes, this is a longer form live report, but your station would likely not have asked you to go live cold if it were not for a special or extended coverage report. This is a less formal, more human, report. You are talking the story here, not reading it to the viewer.

Work with Your Anchor

This is also a good scene for interaction between the reporter and the anchor in the studio. The interaction may help the reporter further focus the report. It may also lend insight to the report. The anchor may see something that the reporter has missed in the live pictures from the scene. The anchor might also be able to relay new information about the scene to the reporter. If the station hears that five more ambulances have been dispatched to the scene, the anchor can report this and the reporter can confirm that the ambulances have arrived, are arriving, or aren't there yet. Then the reporter will be on the lookout for the additional ambulances. The anchor's questions can also give the reporter a brief break from talking. (A chance to grab a quick breath in situations like this is always welcome!)

Keep Moving

It is an amazing feeling to arrive on a scene with seemingly nothing to work with only to realize that you have a wealth of information all around you. You want to do all you can to convey the information without going too far. The viewer knows that you have just arrived on the scene and that it is a rather chaotic situation. He or she is also aware that rescue workers are busy attending to the injured and can't talk to you. No one expects you to have all of the answers at this point. In free-flowing live presentations you are working with what you can see, and you are seeing it as the viewer sees it.

Since you are operating without a safety net in situations like this, don't be surprised if your train of thought gets derailed or switched to another thought track rather quickly. It is natural to hit a bump or two in situations like this. Your goal is always to present your live as cleanly as possible, but don't get rattled by minor mistakes. Keep your mind and mouth moving in cases like this.

If possible, you should try to secure a live interview at the scene. If there is a witness or an official who can give you a couple minutes of their time, grab that person just before your live shot. You can then introduce the scene and point out some of what is going on. Then turn immediately to the live interview subject and add that element to your report. Following the interview, if time permits, you can return for a live updated look at what is going on at the scene. If not, you can wrap immediately.

Make no mistake, notes are an important part of the live presentation. However, a total reliance on notes can be dangerous. It is important to develop your own style. It is important to reach a comfort level in which you can operate with or without notes in any given situation. Keep in mind, there will be cases where you will not be able to make written notes, as in breaking news.

Practicing your live presentations with notes and without notes is a good way to learn how to work well in both cases. You should also work to limit your notes to the essential points you will cover in the live presentation. The talking points will help you organize better and will help give your live report a more natural look, sound, and feel.

4

The Technical Side of Live

The Basics

As a live television news reporter, it is not your job to understand how a live shot works from the technical side of things. Having said that, most reporters will tell you that a basic knowledge of the technical side can be helpful to you in understanding and dealing with the frustration of technical difficulties. It can also help you prevent such failures in certain situations.

Live television news reporters have only limited control over their live presentations. Reporters can control what they say and how they look. The rest is up to the magic of technology and those who are trained to use it. A successful live shot may require as many as ten people. One is the reporter; the other nine are working at the scene and behind the scenes. All of the people and the equipment must be working and working together for the shot to work, so you can see why things sometimes go wrong.

The real basics you are already familiar with. As a live television news reporter, you will either leave the station for your assignment in a live truck or you will meet up with a live truck at your live location. It is from the live truck that we will begin looking at how it all comes together. The live truck is typically one of two vehicles. The first is a large van equipped with a microwave transmitter and dish. The second is a larger truck equipped with a satellite transmitter and dish. There are also trucks with both satellite and microwave technology on board.

Equipment

Microwave Live

The microwave unit is the most commonly used live vehicle in television news today, in large part because it is cheaper to purchase and operate. However, satellite technology is coming down in price, and its use is increasing in popularity. The live microwave unit is basically a mobile television station. The van is often equipped with video editing equipment, television monitors, telephones, intercom systems, audio mixers and speakers, miles of cables and connectors, and the host of other gadgets necessary to make it all work. The principles of live technology are easy to understand, though the systems behind the systems can get very confusing, especially for those who still have trouble getting the VCR clock to stop flashing 12:00.

A live microwave truck has at least one microwave transmitter on board. It also has a retractable mast with a small rotating dish on top. You have probably seen live television news microwave units with the masts fully extended. They look a lot like vans with telephone poles through them. The mast is needed to help the microwave signal get where it is going. Microwave transmission is a line-of-sight proposition. There must be a clear path between the signal coming from the truck and the location where it is to be received.

In Chicago, all stations send their live truck microwave signals in the direction of either the Sears Tower or the John Hancock Building, two of the tallest buildings in the world. Each building is equipped with receivers that pick up the different frequencies. In order to successfully make a live connection, the live signal from the truck must have a clear path to the receiver. As a result, in a large city where there are many potential obstructions, live locations may have to be moved from time to time. This is also true in areas where hills and valleys are common.

The signals sent from the truck are the audio and the video. The video comes directly from the camera being used for the live shot; the audio is from the reporter's microphone. Both signals are routed directly into the truck with cable. The signals are then sent on to the transmitting unit contained in the truck. Each transmitter operates on a different frequency so that stations in the same market do not end up interfering with each other's live shots. When the transmitter is turned on, the signals begin their journey. Attached to the transmitter is a very long cable. This cable, a coiled plastic tubing, snakes around the mast pole and can be as long as fifty-five feet. The tubing runs to the top of the mast and connects to the dish located there.

The hollow, telescoping mast is divided into a number of sections. These sections are typically around six feet in length. The base section is the largest, and each one following is smaller. Air from a compressor, powered by a generator aboard the truck, is injected into the hollowed mast tube sections, forcing them upward. A simple valve keeps the air in when the mast is extended and releases it when the operator wants to lower the mast.

The audio and video signals from the live location travel through the truck and up the mast via the tubing and are aimed and fired at the receiving point by the dish on top of the mast. The dish can rotate left and right; it can also move up and down. This flexibility often allows the operator to fine tune the live shot without having to break down and move the truck to another location.

In most cases, the truck operator will not be able to see the receiving point. This means if the truck is thirty miles from the receiver, it is likely that there will be something that could interfere with the signal. If it is a thirty-foot-tall, three-story building, adjusting the dish upward might do the trick: Remember, the mast is well over thirty feet tall. If the obstacle is taller than that, it may be necessary to find another location for the live shot.

In some cases there is a way around an obstruction even when it is taller than the mast and is in the way of the signal path. As with the balls in billiards, it is sometimes possible to bounce the microwave signal off of certain buildings or objects to redirect the signal onto a clear target path. The signal bounces best off flat and solid portions of a building. Glass does not work as well because it absorbs some of the microwave signal before reflecting the balance of it in the direction of the receiver. The quality of a bounced signal is not the best, but in many cases it is still airable.

In some cases, bouncing will not work. When the obstacles in question are such things as mountains and hills or a forest of tall trees, repeaters are often used to carry the signal to its ultimate destination. In markets where there are too many hills and valleys for live trucks to make direct connections with receiving points, the trucks are all but useless without a way to transfer the signal. In this situation, the use of a repeater is a must. A repeater is basically another receiving sight for the signal. A repeater may be contained on a tower between the live truck and the ultimate destination for the signal. In such a case, the truck signal is aimed at the receiver on the tower. The receiver takes in the signal and processes it; then the audio and video is reamplified and sent on to the main receiving point. In some cases, the repeating station will take in the signal and transmit it to the ultimate destination via a fiber-optic connection.

Fiber-optic connections are becoming more and more popular for handling live signals from hard-to-reach locations or from locations commonly used for live shots. Many professional sports arenas for example, are prewiring their facilities for live television via fiber optics. The video and audio cables are connected to the fiber-optic transmitter. The transmitter converts the signal into a digital form and transmits it by encoded ultraviolet light. It is then received at the station and decoded back into its separate video and audio components. The advantage of fiber-optic transmission is that it does not require line of sight. You can bring many signals into the station at the same time. Microwave can not do this nearly as well because each signal transmitted increases the chance of interference from other locations.

Signals sent out by either microwave or fiber-optic connection will be separated into audio and video components when they arrive at the ultimate receiving point. There, the signals are captured in what is called a *frame synchronizer.* The frame sync compiles the audio and video sources simultaneously. It also times and presents the material simultaneously. The frame sync basically grabs the incoming video and audio and locks them into the same as all house signals, including internal tape machines and cameras.

The live signals may also be routed into other equipment at the station for the live shot. They may be recorded on a video record deck. The video image and sound may also be routed into a number of preview and viewing monitors so anyone who needs to see the live signal can.

Satellite Live

Satellite live is different in many ways from microwave, but the processing and signal use are almost identical. A satellite truck is usually larger than a microwave live unit because the equipment needed for a satellite link is larger in both quantity and size. However, technology is helping to reduce the size and cost of satellite vehicles. Many newer satellites are more portable and can be transported and used in smaller vehicles.

The video and audio signals from a live location are routed into the satellite truck the same way they are in a microwave truck—right from the source. The camera shooting the live shot sends its signal into the truck, and the reporter's microphone is also wired into the truck. The difference is in how the signals get from point A to point B.

The satellite truck does not have a mast, but it does have

a dish. Satellite is not line-of-sight dependent per se. A satellite signal is sent from the truck, or uplinked, into outer space. The signal is received by an orbiting satellite. Here it is processed and sent back down to earth where it is downlinked at the ultimate receiving point. Almost all television stations have downlink capabilities, but not all have or use satellite trucks. Television stations commonly downlink programming from networks and other sources.

Satellite trucks are used most often in markets where the use of microwaves is a hit or miss proposition. They are also used in markets that are geographically expansive. Microwave live trucks have effective ranges of forty miles or less. Satellite trucks can send up a signal from anywhere. Once that signal is received at a station, it is processed and routed the same way that microwave is.

Communication

Communication is the key to bringing all of the people and technology together to pull off a live shot. Communication begins at the point of the live shot. It is here that the truck operator, the reporter, and the photojournalist must be on the same page. The reporter and photographer will discuss how the live shot will be presented. Any camera movements such as a pan away from the reporter to a point of interest must be discussed in advance. Failure to do so might lead to problems on air. The photojournalist will then work with the truck operator in setting up the live location. This will include camera placement, lighting, and equipment wiring. In union shops these duties are clearly drawn up and divided.

Tuning In

The truck operator is responsible for putting up the mast, firing up the transmitter and tuning in the signal. Tuning in the signal requires the operator to be in touch with someone at the ultimate receiving destination who is in a position to visually monitor the signal. That person is usually an electronic news gathering (ENG) operator. In this case, the ENG operator is gathering the truck signal. When the signal is sent from the truck and received, it may be of poor quality. If this is the case, the dish needs to be moved to a better position. The ENG operator will then instruct the truck operator to manipulate the dish in an effort to improve signal quality. If this is not possible, the ENG operator may instruct the truck operator to move the live location and try from another site.

The ENG operator is concerned about the quality of both the video and audio signals. Since the two signals are separated when they arrive at the receiving point, it is entirely possible to have very good video and bad audio, or vice versa. If there is a problem, the ENG operator must notify the truck operator, who in turn will discuss it with the photographer. In the case of audio problems, a microphone or cable at the live location may be to blame, and replacing the cable or microphone may solve the problem. If the cable and microphone are fine, it could be a problem with the truck's audio mixer. The truck operator will check the mixer. If the mixer is okay, the trouble may be far worse: The audio problem may be in the transmitter itself. In that case, the live shot is probably doomed, and the truck will head back to the station to be checked by an engineer.

Reporter to Station (Mix-minus Mix-ups)

The truck operator and ENG operator must also work together to ensure that the communication line between the station and the reporter is made. This is accomplished with a system known as interruptible foldback (IFB). Live television reporters carry with them specially molded earpieces which are wired into an IFB system. The IFB connects the station and the reporter, usually via a telephone line. The reporter's earpiece wire is connected to another cable in the field which routes it into the an integrated telephone interface system in the truck. The truck operator dials a special number linked to the station. This line is a mixer output (the mix-minus) of the station's on-air output minus the audio of the person listening to it. That is to say, the reporter can hear the anchor through his or her earpiece, just as the viewer at home can, but when the reporter is live he or she can't hear his or her own voice through the earpiece. The configuration of the IFB system also allows the producer or director to press a button in the control room and talk to the reporter before air or while on air if necessary. The reporter and the truck operator can hear what is being said over the IFB system.

This is how things work under ideal circumstances. There are a number of cases, though, where the reporter in the field hears more than he or she would like. On occasion, mix-minus problems occur, and the the reporter hears himself or herself through the IFB system earpiece. When this occurs, it can really send the reporter into a tailspin. When you have a mix-minus mix-up, the reporter is hearing his or herself a second or so delayed. The result is an incredibly loud, annoying, and very distracting echo in the ear.

A reporter operating with such an echo has a very hard time keeping a real-time delivery because people naturally listen through an echo before proceeding. This is often referred to as the Grand Canyon effect. Since the echo occurs right at the beginning of the live shot, it is very likely the reporter will become startled and stumble. This is one very important reason to have everything tested and retested long before the live shot takes place if at all possible. The reporter's IFB cable is usually kept in a pocket. This means that in a pinch, a reporter who recognizes a problem with the mix-minus can quickly reach down and pull the plug on his or her IFB cable and continue with the live shot. It is important to note that while this will take care of the echo for the report, the producer and director will not be able to directly communicate instructions to the reporter.

Just about every reporter has a mix-minus nightmare; just ask veteran TV newsman Greg Prather:

> I once had to do a live shot for NBC network news. This was a day after the Gulf War started. I was at a New Orleans grade school where teachers were trying to explain the war to the children. NBC learned about the story and wanted to include my report in their nonstop coverage. The satellite truck arrived at the school, I got hooked up and everything seemed fine. As it turned out, there was one big problem, the mix-minus. I didn't have it, and it made everything so awkward. I was hearing everything seconds later from the anchor in New York. The whole live shot on network television turned out to be a real disaster. I was interviewing children live, and I had no videotape or anything to fall back on. I looked at the tale of the live shot later, and I came to the conclusion that no one looked stupid except me. I had no

control over the situation, what could I do? New York was in control. I did the best I could under the circumstances, but it was very, very awkward. Compounding the embarrassment, I told my family and friends from across the country that I was going to be live on national television. Of course, they all watched.

Glitches Happen

Over the course of your career, you will find that there are any number of technical glitches that will disrupt, mess up, or even lead to the cancellation of your live shot. There is absolutely nothing you can do in these cases. This can be frustrating, but you must be prepared for anything to happen.

One concern in particular is lightning. Each year in this business, someone is injured or killed in a live shot accident related to lightning. This is a very important consideration when covering stories where threatening weather is in the immediate area. The reason that lightning poses such a hazard with respect to microwave live units is the mast: The mast is little more than a metal or composite pole sticking up fifty feet in the air. It is essentially screaming, "Hey, hit me!" If lightning strikes the mast of a live truck it will travel down into and around the truck. The strike will injure or kill anyone in the truck, touching the truck, or, in some cases, even those near the truck.

Most news operations have strict guidelines for bad weather live shots. They typically order the truck operator to drop the mast at the first hint of lightning in the area. It may be far off, but there is no way of knowing exactly how far away it is or how fast the storm is moving it toward the truck.

In the interest of getting a story on the air, some news directors or executive producers have been known to encourage crews to wait as long as they can before pulling the plug. This is wrong. The crew in the field is in the best position to determine the severity of the situation and should be in control when it comes to making the final call under these conditions. Never let anyone force you to go ahead with a live shot in conditions that might very well put your life in jeopardy.

There are, of course, many less dangerous events that can cause you problems. Cameras will break, microphones will conk out, live trucks will break down, and signals will bounce to nowhere. Get used to it. Glitches are a fact of life and a part of this career. Ranting and raving or pointing the finger at someone will do nothing to help the situation; it can only make things worse.

In many cases, the story you lose to technical difficulties will be a very good one. These are the toughest to deal with. Intense reporters who are running on adrenaline hate running into brick walls at full speed. That is exactly what it feels like to have a potentially awesome live shot trashed because some two-dollar connector no longer connects you to the station. Hang in there, it happens to all of us.

5

Finding Your Balance

Learning from Failure

Even the best, most confident live television news reporters will fail from time to time. The best of the best will chew on words, forget where they are going with a story, or ignore or blow a roll cue. One thing you must face as a young reporter is the fact that you will fall on your face on live television many times over your career. It is how you handle failure that will determine how long your career will last. The reality is that you are human, and no matter how skilled or polished or practiced you are, failures are inevitable. Having said that, it is important to put failure into perspective so you can turn an otherwise negative situation into a positive growing experience.

If there is one individual who is identified with success, it is superstar basketball player Michael Jordan. There is little question that Michael Jordan is the best player to ever step on a basketball court. Jordan holds championship rings, most valuable player honors, all-star honors, and league records; he is also the reason a hall of fame exists in this sport. Most people would never associate the word fail-

ure with Michael Jordan. But he would, and that is why
Jordan is what he is today. This point is made crystal clear
in a very special advertising spot created by NIKE, Inc., for
whom Jordan has been a long-time spokesperson. The ad
is called "9,000 Shots" and features Michael Jordan ex-
plaining a number of the personal pitfalls that helped build
the character he needed to get to the top.

> I've missed more than 9,000 shots in my career.
> I've lost almost 300 games.
> 26 times, I've been trusted to take the game winning
> shot, and missed.
> I failed over, and over, and over again in my life.
> And that is why I succeed.

It doesn't get any clearer or more powerful than that. The
ability to rebound from adversity and reach the top in spite
of it all is the hallmark of all great people, in all career fields.

Many live television careers end before they really begin.
Stress and failure and are among the top reasons many decide this business is not for them. Stress, in particular, is responsible for the early demise not only of many promising
careers, but also of marriages and friendships. Health problems and drug and alcohol addictions are also often a direct
result of the inability to handle the stresses this career
places on individuals on a regular basis. Every job has its
moments. Stress is everywhere. However, no field can compare in stress intensity to the constant deadline and demanding live performance aspects of television news. It is
for that reason that learning how to manage stress and
learning from failure can make you a better reporter and a
healthier, happier person.

Since most habits, bad and good, are picked up in the early stages of career development, this is the ideal time and forum in which to discuss some of the things you can do to be the best you can be. The goal is to help you to recognize self-defeating behavior patterns that will lead to trouble. As with any medical condition, prevention is always the best medicine. If a problem does exist already, early detection means a better chance for long-term survival.

Every bookstore in the country is stocked with titles that deal with stress and with self-help and other ways to cure our ills. The goal here is not to dive deeply into these areas, but to air some issues that may not receive enough attention among television news professionals. These issues go to the heart of being able to cope on the job. Dealing with life's stresses is an individual issue. There are, however, a number of important adjustments and changes in both thought and action that seem to work wonders on people across the board. Many of the thoughts and ideas in this chapter come from friends and professionals who have found the answers only after having made the mistakes. They have failed, and learning from their failures can help you stay on track.

Stress and Adrenaline

Stress these days is treated as if it were a four-letter word. The truth of the matter is that stress can be helpful to you as a live television news reporter. It can also kill you and your career. How can something so good be so bad and so bad be so good?

You have no doubt heard of adrenaline. This chemical is released into your system by the adrenal glands under stressful situations, usually negative situations such as those in which you may be in danger. The adrenaline causes your heart rate to increase and the blood flow to be directed toward your muscles. In most cases, the body begins to perspire. At this point the natural fight or flight response is in high gear. The brain needs a certain level of adrenaline to keep the system energized. A lack of adrenaline can literally take the gas out of you. Low adrenaline levels lead to exhaustion, fatigue, and a general slowdown of your system. This is not a good condition to be in when preparing for or executing a live television performance.

Positive stress gives us the boost we need to rise to the occasion and to be the best we can be. The stress of coming in just under deadline when most think you won't can be a real charge. The stress of landing a lead story exclusive when no one else could is a pure rush. The stress of arriving on a chaotic breaking news scene and walking and talking the viewer through it all is as close to a high as you can get without a court date. Stress in these situations gives your body a surge of adrenaline—that rush that helps bring you to a higher level. Many in this business are drawn to it for that very reason. The adrenaline surge in many cases energizes, improves performance, sharpens focus, and builds confidence. This is all good. The trouble comes in when one becomes addicted to the positive stress response and/or when a number negative stress factors exist at the same time.

Extremes: Living without Balance

Negative Stressors

You can probably think of one hundred different things that produce negative stress. Negative stress is the car payment due yesterday. It is the unexpected meeting with the boss over a pretty big mistake—one you made. Weather conditions can be stressful in a less than positive manner. Smoking and drinking can add significant stress to your system. Chemical imbalances are known to play a role in stress. Major events in your life such as a move or a major debt purchase can weigh in heavily in the stress department. Fights or arguments with a husband, wife, mother, father, sister, brother, neighbor, coworker, boss, or stranger can be stressful. Death and taxes are also a concern. Pushing your body and mind too hard too often is a major negative stressor. Let us begin at the end, since overworking the system seems to be a part of this field and a big part of the problem.

Work Addiction

The demands of live television news never fade. Younger reporters who have no shortage of energy but lack experience are prime candidates for early burnout in this field. Television news is not a nine to five business. When you start out in this field you give up weekends, holidays, and normal hours willingly. Your goal is to get the experience you need to move on to the next level, the next market, the next pay scale. There is absolutely nothing wrong with this kind of drive and determination if you have both focus and balance.

Focus in this discussion is defined as a clear picture of what you want to do and where you want to do it. It is the driving force of most young reporters. Whether it is a major market, a network, or landing the main reporter–anchor job at your hometown station, there is a goal. This field tends to draw to it people who are willing to sacrifice a lot, if not everything else in life, to achieve "the goal." That willingness to sacrifice tends to shift life out of balance, and the absence of balance is where trouble begins.

It is not uncommon for young reporters, and veterans for that matter, to put in workdays that far exceed the hours of most career positions. Some work ten hours, others routinely put in up to sixteen hours a day. Most people work to live; many journalists, though, live to work. There is no question that the news of the day and many special assignments will require you to work long hours. This is normal. When you work extended hours for extended periods of time, however, you are heading down a dangerous path.

The math is pretty simple. If you are spending up to two-thirds of your day at work and about a third of your day asleep, you are living to work. This means you have allocated no time for friends, family, relationships, exercise, shopping, hobbies, or relaxation. Maybe, if you are lucky, you can cram it all into the weekend.

Let's add a few other thoughts into the mix. When you are a live television news reporter, you are on the move more often than not. You move from one story to another quickly and with little downtime. You also have little time to pick a nice restaurant for a well-balanced lunch or dinner, or both. The fast-paced life of a live television news reporter often means fast food as well. It is quick, cheap, and you can eat it in the car or live truck at a high rate of speed as you move from one scene to another. Maybe you are called to a story where there isn't even a fast food restaurant around. Hostage situations require you to remain stationary for hours on end, and if you haven't eaten, you likely won't for a long time. Who is thinking about food, anyway, when news is happening? No one, and that is the point: It is not uncommon for reporters caught up in their work to forget about eating altogether.

There are days where you will be at that hostage situation for hours. You will forget to eat or will be unable to do so for one reason or another. You'll get home late at night, and all of a sudden discover two very important things. One, you are starving. Two, you are wired. The adrenaline rush from the story will keep you up. This means you will overeat and won't be able to sleep until very early in the morning. Your sleep schedule has been altered again, but your work schedule has not. You must be back in the office several hours earlier now.

Can you feel the negative stresses building, ever so slowly? Let us keep going. Add a little caffeine to keep you alert and maybe some nicotine to give you that kick you need before and after a story.

The human body and mind can only take so much abuse. Sooner or later a lack of sleep, poor nutrition, environmental factors, lack of exercise, lack of relationships, and everything else will catch up with you. You will, at that point, realize that your life is dangerously out of balance. This can happen quickly. Many reporters in their mid-twenties and up are confronted by this reality. Please note that a reporter must always work hard, should always give one hundred percent effort to every story. At the same time, recognize that you can push yourself too far for your own good. This can only have a negative impact on your performance and on your life.

As a reporter, one of your main responsibilities is to show balance in your work. You should never give too much time or attention in your report to one side or issue over another. Unfortunately, as you can see, that is not always true in the lives of newspeople. To function best, you should always try to check your personal life at the door when you arrive at work, and pick it back up when you leave. The lack of balance in life makes this very difficult for many reporters. This is, in part, because many do not maintain any real life outside of work. Many of those who do make the time to socialize outside of work often do so almost exclusively with coworkers or others who work in the same field. Both of these cases represent unhealthy behavior.

Early on, you may be able to handle everything. You can deal with the schedule. You are able to forget about holidays and special occasions for the most part because you are focused on your work. You can put off dates or social occasions because you are building for the future. You can skip outings with friends because you are paying your dues. Someday, when everything is right, you will pick up the phone and instantly restore balance to your life. Not likely. You see, at that point, you are ready to move on to the next rung of the ladder, the next market, the next pay scale, the next ... next.

At the new location, you start over again as the new kid on the block. You get the worst schedule. You work all holidays and most weekends. You don't have to worry about friends because you don't know anyone and, frankly, you won't have time to meet them anyway. So you spend most of your day working news. You go out with the people you work with and talk about news. You go home and maybe eat something (if you forgot to earlier), go to bed, wake up, and do it all over again. Make no mistake, you are your decisions. Those decisions will catch up with you down the road if you are not careful. Many reporters and anchors will tell you that if they could do anything differently, it would be to manage stress and balance life better than they have.

Chronic Stress

Over time, your body and mind learn to handle a lot of stress. In many cases, though, stress overload causes mental and physiological reactions that can be dangerous at best, fatal at worst. Chronic stress is one of the most significant health problems in the United States. On average, job stress is considered to be near the top when it comes to aggravating factors. That being the average, live television is miles above the scale.

Chronic stress can lead to a host of major medical problems. Heart disease is most often associated with long-term exposure to stress. Stress also takes its toll on energy and on the ability to function at one's best. Under stressful situations, many people lose energy and experience fatigue. If that is not enough, stress and a bad reporter's diet can contribute to a host of gastrointestinal problems. Headaches and backaches are also common by-products of prolonged exposure to stress. Instead of addressing the root causes of stress, many opt to self-medicate. Live television news reporting has more than its share of people who use and abuse both drugs and alcohol. Much of that can be tied to job stress compounded by life (or lack of a life) stresses.

The story subject matter also plays a key role in stress and response. Just covering a tragic story or series of stories can take its toll. Dealing with death and with grieving family and friends is tough. Add in police who are not helping your story and a crowd of onlookers who aren't necessarily thrilled that you are shooting all of this and you have a pretty stressful ordeal. You want to be at your best and sharpest when operating under these circumstances. If you didn't sleep well the night before, if you didn't eat well last night or this morning, or if you are in poor physical shape, your edge is reduced. If you were drinking the night before, odds are you are not as sharp as you should be. If you have the breakup of a relationship due to your commitment to work on your mind, you are not as sharp as you should be. If you are dealing with a combination of the above, ask yourself what kind of job you can really do. The answer is pretty simple. Your long-hours approach to work is admirable, but over the long haul it has had a negative impact on you as a whole and on your ability to do the job you were hired to do.

Imagine that a star athlete puts in sixteen hours of practice a day, working to be the best he can be. Imagine that the player doesn't eat right, sleep well, maintain healthy relationships, have fun, live life. How well do you think he will perform over the long run? Without balance there is trouble.

Panic Attacks

Many reporters can live an overstressed life for a long time before it becomes a professional issue. Some, however reach a point at which they can no longer go on. One day all of the stress, work and personal, comes to a head. It often happens live, on air. The reporter or anchor suddenly has a shortness of breath and can't get his or her words out. Others feel hot flashes and are on the edge of passing out. The symptoms in many respects mirror a heart attack. This is an attack, but not of the heart. This is a full-blown panic attack.

You won't hear much talk about panic attacks in newsrooms. That is because many who have them never tell coworkers about them. Panic attacks are very real and potentially devastating. They won't kill you, but they have killed a number of promising careers. A panic attack is like throwing the engines of a plane at cruising speed into reverse. An anchor or reporter who has performed well for years suddenly can't speak. The red light on the studio camera freezes a veteran anchor like a deer in the headlights. The field reporter stumbles and, instead of moving on as he normally does, can't get past the mistake. The heart races. Sweat pours down the face. Breathing becomes shallow and difficult. The reporter or anchor freezes in place. Cool and confident feelings on air are replaced by dizziness and nausea. Fear feeds on fear in cases like this. Reporters and anchors who have performed on demand for so many years without so much as a hint of a problem are now all but paralyzed. Years and layers of stress have finally taken control. The body and mind have finally given in to the reality that fatigue and exhaustion can be overpowering.

It sounds a lot like fiction, but more reporters and anchors suffer from panic attacks than you might imagine. Even those with seemingly flawless deliveries are not immune to panic attacks. Some of the most cocky reporters and anchors are quite humbled by the realization that they are less than perfect on air and in life. There are few if any symptoms leading up to an attack. One-time events can lead to panic attacks, but that is not typical. Usually panic attacks are the result of a lot of different types of stress building up over time. One day, enough is enough, and over the edge you go.

More often than not, the panic attack is a result of work stresses and personal stresses combined. The lion's share of the blame goes to those things outside of work that you fail to handle properly or chose to ignore altogether. Panic attacks mean the end of a career for many. The panic tends to feed off of itself. Once an individual has suffered a panic attack, he or she fears the repeat of an attack. This gives rise to the fear that an attack will occur the next time he or she is on air. Thus the problem perpetuates itself and undermines the self-confidence of even the most confident reporter or anchor. In the end, the individual will give in to the panic attack and leave television news. In other cases, the individual will seek help.

Since the physiological symptoms of panic attacks are numerous and often mimic heart attacks, many sufferers seek medical help. Only after testing is it confirmed that the individual is in fact suffering from a panic-related disorder. At this point, the person can begin to address the problems and life deficiencies that led to the attacks. The cure for this problem often involves a combination of psychological and other medical approaches, but panic attacks can be beaten. More importantly, they can be avoided, as can most of the other problems we have touched on to this point in the chapter. The answers are easier than you might imagine. It is important, however, to grasp the important concepts before they reach the problematic level.

Finding the Balance: Managing Stress

In many cases, simple changes in diet and lifestyle can reduce stresses across the board. Having said that, these types of changes can be among the most difficult to make. Most of us have built and maintained bad habits for years. See how many of the following statements you would agree with.

- I often enjoy certain foods that aren't good for me.
- I smoke cigarettes.
- I drink too much alcohol.
- I start my day with caffeine—coffee, colas, etc.—and need a caffeine boost several times a day to function at my best.
- I don't get enough sleep.
- I don't exercise nearly enough.
- I don't eat three meals a day. When I do eat, it is not really a balanced diet. I don't know much about proper nutrition.

If you can relate to one or more of these statements, there is room in your life for improvement, for the type of improvement that will help reduce your stress level, improve your health, and make you feel better in every way. Let's look at how and why.

Caffeine

The only thing more important than a camera in a newsroom is the coffeemaker. In fact, many newsrooms are equipped with the heavy duty, tandem warmer, nonstop coffee well. In many cases, newspeople drink coffee not by the cup, but by the pot. The first couple of cups get the mind and heart going at the beginning of a shift. The next several help keep the edge. There is nothing wrong with a cup or two of coffee—per day, that is. Caffeine is a central nervous system stimulant. Many veteran newspeople will tell you that too much caffeine over time can lead to health problems and impact your live performance. After more than a couple of cups of coffee, caffeine begins to boost the level of adrenaline in the system. The heart and respiration rates increase considerably. Many believe that caffeine gives them an energy boost. The truth is that caffeine can actually rob your system of energy. The rush of adrenaline caused by the ingestion of high amounts of caffeine is countered by a crash, or loss of energy, when the adrenaline high wears off. At this point, the reaction is generally to go back to the coffee pot for another "boost of energy."

Coffee is by no means the only significant source of caffeine that you will encounter in the course of your day. Almost all soft drinks are loaded with caffeine. Chocolate is another favorite pick-me-up. Even some medications contain caffeine. It is easy to understand why most people get more caffeine than they need each day. It is also easy to see

why this is not a good thing for the live television news reporter. The increased adrenaline alone is a reason to avoid
too much caffeine. The chemical reaction adds stress to an
already stressful environment. You don't need an increased
heart rate, altered breathing, or more nervous energy when
your are under stress.

If you could quit caffeine altogether you would be better off, but most of us either can't or won't do it. This is
where balance makes all the difference in the world. Learn
to moderate your caffeine intake. If you have two cups of
coffee in the morning, don't have a caffeine-loaded soft
drink with lunch. Try water or juice instead. If you love
chocolate, learn to love coffee less or learn to love the caf-
feine-free variety. If you drink too much coffee, try mixing
the regular caffeinated variety with the decaffeinated. Caf-
feine-free soft drinks are growing in popularity; if you are a
soda junky, alternate between caffeinated and noncaf-
feinated soda. There are any number of combinations that
can help you reduce your daily caffeine intake. The key is
to be conscious of how much you are taking in on a regular basis and how it is impacting your life and work.

Alcohol

Another commonly used and abused pick-me-up (or let-
me-down) is alcohol. It goes without saying that if you
need an eye-opener or two in the morning before work you
might have a problem. Likewise, if you drink while on the
job because you think it will relax you or enhance your performance, you are heading for trouble. Some in this high
stress field use alcohol to take the edge off after work or to
forget a particularly gruesome or troubling news event that

day. This behavior can also become problematic. Caffeine is a stimulant, alcohol is a depressant. Alcohol works to numb the brain as an anesthetic would. As with caffeine, there is some research that indicates a drink or two a day might not be that bad. But too much alcohol too often is shown to pose significant health risks.

Having a beer or a glass of wine after a tough day is not uncommon in this field. The problem is, the more you drink to escape or reduce stress, the more you drink. Live television news is rarely without stress. Over time, the glass of wine you drink to unwind becomes two glasses. As your stress level increases, your drinking is likely to increase, as is your tolerance. When alcohol tolerance goes up, the amount of alcohol required to reach the same high increases. Soon, what started as one glass of wine becomes two, then three, then half a bottle on its way to becoming empty.

At the same time, the increase in alcohol consumption is taking a significant toll on the body. Alcohol is a toxin or poison, and poisons are stressors. Alcohol poisons the liver, in particular. It destroys liver cells, and over time it can destroy the entire organ. The death of the liver from alcohol is an all too common cause of death in this country, but the liver is not the only part of the body alcohol can destroy. The heart is impacted by heavy drinking over time, and the stomach and gastrointestinal system can be damaged beyond repair due to chronic alcohol abuse.

Physical problems aside, excess drinking can have a devastating impact on your career and personal life. You no doubt know someone or know of someone who has misused alcohol for a long time. Think about how that person's life has changed and how your perception of that person has changed because of the alcohol problem. This is a stressful field, one that requires you to be in peak form if you want to succeed. It is only a matter of time before alcohol problems begin to impact performance. Drinking problems are not always obvious to others. Many who drink to take the edge off night after night can sleep it off and go into work the next day, seemingly normal. But make no mistake, if you have a problem that you have been hiding from others, it will come out eventually. The camera never lies.

As a live television news reporter, you will often witness firsthand the destructive power of alcohol. You will cover prom night stories where a couple of promising students are killed because they were drinking and driving or because someone else was. You will respond to domestic disputes. Some will be battery, and some will be murder, and alcohol will be a contributing factor in a significant percentage of these cases. Barroom brawls that lead to violence or death are often the result of intoxicated patrons getting out of hand. Alcohol impairs judgment. Alcohol reduces inhibitions. Alcohol contributes to both accidental and intentional deaths every day. It makes very little sense to spend your day covering a tragic or gruesome death tied to alcohol use and then go home and bury yourself in a bottle. Again, moderation and balance are key. Certainly you should enjoy yourself. You should drink responsibly. As a news reporter you are taught to ask who, what, when, where, why, and how. When it comes to alcohol consumption, it doesn't hurt to ask yourself a few of those questions. Examine when, where, why, and how much you drink. If you think you have a problem, you probably do. Help is readily available; if you need it, get it before it destroys your life.

Smoking

Newsrooms, like most other places of business are becoming nonsmoking environments. The health problems associated with smoking are well known. Even the tobacco giants are themselves acknowledging the problems. Cigarette smoke can be the source of serious health trouble for the smoker and nonsmoker alike, and secondhand smoke is now recognized as a significant health threat to nonsmokers.

Smoking is linked to a host of cancers, from the lungs to the bladder. Smoking also leads to heart disease. There are literally hundreds of chemicals in each cigarette, the most significant of which is nicotine. Nicotine is the reason many people can't quit smoking and the reason those who do have such a hard time kicking the habit. Nicotine is believed to be among the most addictive drugs known to man. Some studies have suggested that it is even more addictive than heroine and cocaine. It has been called the perfect drug because the rate of inhalation can have opposite effects on the body and brain. The cigarette can be used to jump-start or stimulate the smoker; this is why many smokers light up as soon as they wake up. It can also slow things down, giving the smoker a calming sensation; this is why many smokers light up before going to bed.

This may be the one exception to the theory of balance in everything. Here there is no room for balance. It is proven that smoking kills. Along the way, smoking can cause problems with your voice and with your breathing. You are likely to become sicker more often and remain ill longer if you are a smoker. All of these things work against your performance as a live television news reporter. Coughing and hacking on the air does little to improve your standing with the audience. In many cases, the smoker's voice sounds more and more unhealthy because it is. And if you are sick more frequently than a nonsmoker, someone else is out there doing the live report you would otherwise do. Who knows, that might be a career-making story.

Many are concerned that quitting smoking will lead to weight gain. This is especially true in television, where those on camera already seem to carry ten or so extra pounds. Weight, however, can be managed with exercise and diet. If you are a smoker, one of the single best things you can do for yourself and your career is to call it quits right now. There are more aids available to help you quit than ever before. Many are available over the counter, and others are available by prescription. It doesn't matter how you quit. It only matters that you do.

Exercise

A small amount of exercise can go a long way in reducing stress and increasing your level of physical fitness. Television news schedules make it difficult to exercise regularly. Although long hours reduce the chances that any free time will be spent exercising, few people need the benefits of exercise more than live television news reporters. Exercise is the physical route to mental health. It tones the body and clears the mind and is an important part of every day's routine. Exercise has also been shown to reduce worry and increase positive thinking and self-esteem.

Medical studies have indicated that thirty minutes of aerobic exercise taken three times a week can extend and increase the quality of life. Exercise is a lifestyle element; it is something you must adopt as a regular part of your life. Getting started is easy, but it is important to note that talking with your doctor before taking up a new exercise routine is always advised.

Remember, few people really enjoy exercise for itself, but they do enjoy seeing the results of their hard work. Noticing an increase in muscle mass, a reduction in fat, and more stamina are among the most significant rewards. A reduction in stress and a more positive attitude also tend to follow a good exercise routine. It is important to start exercising by doing something you enjoy. This could be riding a bicycle, in-line skating, or jogging. If you like at least part of your workout, it is bound to be more effective, and you are likely to stick with it. It will also make the other parts of your workouts—sit-ups, for example—a little more bearable. The last thing you want to do is hate working out or dread doing certain exercises. Just remember, like most things in life, short-term pains are rewarded with long-term gains.

Health clubs are a good place to begin your quest for a sound body and mind. Many television personalities like the idea of working out in public clubs. Others though do not like the recognition factor when they are out of makeup and working up a sweat. Some prefer home gyms.

Equipment is affordable and is as good, in many cases, as that you will find at a health club.

Whatever you do, warm up before exercise and cool down after it. It is helpful to add weight training to your exercise program as well. You may want to consult a trainer to help determine what program is best for you. A trainer can help evaluate where you are and let you know what it will take to get to where you want to be. A trainer can also help with nutrition questions and show you the proper techniques and forms to follow when performing specific exercises.

All this sounds good, but none of it addresses the time factor: You have to make the time. Exercise is a commitment to yourself and your well-being and you must learn to make the commitment to yourself. This is part of the whole idea of balance. Set realistic goals for yourself and force yourself to find the time to make them happen. This may mean you get up an hour earlier than you want to. It may mean you change into sweats right after work and head to the gym. Find the time. It is there. Many people can spend a half hour telling you all the reasons they can't find time to exercise: If they can find that much time to tell you about it, they can find the time to exercise.

There are also things you can do in the course of your work day that will help. On-the-job exercising is a good habit. If you have an interview on the third floor of a building, take the stairs instead of the elevator. Park your news car farther away from instead of closer to where you are going. This will allow you a brisk walk, and it might reduce the number of parking lot dings your car is subjected to.

Any time you can increase the amount of walking you do in a day, you are helping yourself get in shape.

The good news is that many news stations are recognizing the benefits of exercise. Some stations have equipment on site that employees can use before or after work. Others have discounted health club memberships at local facilities. Still more will offer health club memberships as a benefit when it comes to contract negotiations.

As you can see, there are a number of exercise options available. You need to find the ones that work for you. Make a commitment to fitness. Reduce your stress. Increase your happiness and improve your outlook on life. Enjoy all of the benefits that come with getting in shape. Your career will benefit from the move. Your life will change for the better.

Diet

If the old saying "You are what you eat" is true, many reporters are little more than greasy burgers and junk food. The live television news reporter rarely has time to sit down and enjoy a well-balanced, nutritious meal. The reality of this job is that dinner consists of a "number one with a diet" from a local drive-through. The dashboard dinner is okay from time to time, but not as frequently as many reporters make it. A poor diet will impact your energy level, your health, your weight, and your performance. Without the proper fuel, the body can not function at peak levels. Consistently poor nutrition can lead to health problems. It is as easy to get into bad eating habits as it is to not find the time to exercise. Here again, you must work to make the necessary changes and focus on how much you and your career will benefit in the long run.

Many young reporters start bad eating habits when they start their first job. Deadlines force many to find a quick fix for hunger pains or grumbling stomachs: a candy bar here, a bag of chips there, and a couple cans of soda to wash it all down. Such junk food can certainly fill an empty stomach. The trouble is, it is being filled with junk. To be at your peak as a live television news reporter, you need to be alert and focused. This is difficult if your system lacks energy. The key is finding a way to get the type of food you need to function while staying away from the stuff that will drag you down.

As a rule, fast food is not healthy. It is generally loaded with fat, and the "low fat" versions still contain a lot of fat. Most of these foods are fried. They certainly taste good, but they do little to help boost your energy or health. The only thing they will boost over time is your cholesterol level. You should get in the habit of bringing food to work with you when you can. A packed lunch from home is generally healthier and in some cases cheaper than dining out all of the time. This also allows you to eat when you feel you need to. You should also pack some healthy snacks with you for times when you need more energy.

Fruits like apples and bananas will give you a nutritious pick-me-up without filling you with junk you don't need. Vegetables like carrots are easy to package and carry. They also provide nutrients instead of empty calories. Your goal is to keep fats to a minimum and increase the amount of protein and carbohydrates in your daily diet. There is no shortage of books that can provide simple recipes for good eating. There are plenty of web sites as well that can help guide you to the right foods.

Relaxation

One of the best things you can do to help boost your career and live performance is to forget all about it. That's right. There is nothing better for you than being able to put aside work and pick up something else in your life. The truth of the matter is that you can not function for a long period of time in a one-dimensional life. If work is all you have, you are in real trouble. It is okay to be focused. It is great to be committed. And going above and beyond the call of duty on a regular basis in this career is expected. But the ideal of living, sleeping, and eating any job is really silly.

You will find that learning to relax means learning to let go of the stresses of work. It means focusing your attention on other things and other people in your life. It is about the little things in life that make you happy. It is a hobby, a long weekend, a date, a good movie. It is about cooking and polishing your car. It is about spending some of that hard-earned money on silly things. It is about a home, family, your spouse, girlfriend, boyfriend. The things that matter most in life are usually not associated with work. Few reporters want their resume on their tombstone. In finding balance, you find understanding. That understanding helps you put things into perspective. That perspective helps you become better at everything you do. So, you see, forgetting about work for a while can actually make you that much better at it.

Balance is not something you can seek once in a while. You must learn to find it in everyday life. If you are so focused on work that everything else is blurred, you have a false sense of life. You are more inclined to beat yourself up over small mistakes or failures you encounter along the way if you lack the perspective balance brings. Failures are difficult enough to deal with. Blowing them out of proportion only increases the likelihood that they will occur again. Understanding failures comes from understanding the role they play in life and the role they play in achieving success.

It is often difficult to see the big picture when you are just starting out in this field. Your focus is on proving yourself. Your drive is to climb the market ladder. You want to be bigger and better than the best. What you come to realize is that the best live television news reporters are the ones who have made the changes necessary in life to understand it better.

You have an advantage. There is a wealth of advice and information available to you on improving your life and skills. The best advice is to take advantage of it all. Recognize those things that will help you in both the short term and the long run. Just as you try to emulate the styles of those you admire on television, pattern your life and behaviors after successful examples and proven formulas.

Stress is a fact of life. Failure is a fact of life. The amazing thing is that although they both can be negative and even fatal, they can also be positive and inspirational. It is up to you to decide what they will mean for your life and for your career.

6

Practice! Practice! Practice!

Why Practice?

Becoming a good live television news reporter takes time and practice. There are no real "naturals" in this field; there are only those who are more comfortable than others with the live presentation. One of the best ways to increase your comfort level and confidence is by practicing. It may sound strange, but you can practice live television news reporting. Doing so requires you to open your mind and challenges you to use your imagination and your observation skills.

Practicing the presentation is becoming an important addition to broadcast journalism programs at many of the top universities and colleges around the nation. This is true not only at schools that have either live television news capabilities or access to local television stations, but also at a large number of schools that do not. Practice brings together all aspects of the student's education and teaches students how to apply the ideas and principles they have learned in a realistic setting. Northwestern University professor Patricia Dean explains how practice is incorporated into the program at the university, one of the top journalism schools in the country.

Here at Northwestern University we teach journalism. What I find though for most students is that the most intimidating part [of television journalism] is the performance aspect. The big thing that I tell [students] is that they just have to practice .... The only way to do it is just to do it. In a college or university you can [practice] in a relatively safe environment. In the classroom here we say we are live. In the worst case, you screw up or break down and just can't finish .... In this setting, it is just like falling off a horse. We put you right back on and say "just do it." Ironically, in front of their peers [performance] appears to present more pressure. I encourage [students] to prepare, then ask them to just tell me the story. Tell it to me in a way that it is easy for me to understand it. What I concentrate [on] is the journalism aspect of it. Some problems that are nerve related will go away. If I don't have [students] practice what is wrong and emphasize what is right, they make a lot of progress.

Practice will make you more comfortable in organizing and presenting your thoughts. It will also help you move forward when you make mistakes instead of losing your train of thought and getting stuck. Practice will show you how well, or poorly, you have put a story together. Practice will also help sharpen your ability to think on your feet and talk at the same time. There are any number of ways to practice live television, but one of the best is to create a scenario based on a series of facts, then assemble and present a story.

Using Practice Scenarios

Start with the Basics

The practice scenario can be one based either on a real news event or on one that you have created. You can vary the urgency of the situation as well. Your news scene might be a breaking news piece like a plane crash. It might also be a live entertainment report where your favorite celebrities are arriving at an awards banquet. You should try a variety of situations and change the style of the presentation each time.

If you are modeling your scene after a real news event, you might want to try re-creating an actual report: Watch the lead story on your local or national newscast. Listen very closely to the anchor lead and the reporter's live presentation. Take notes, watch the pictures, and listen to the sound. When the report is over, turn off the television set and re-create the scene and report.

The living room is usually a good place to do the re-creation. It is large and generally has a number of items you can use as props to help explain your story. If the story is about a plane crash, use the living room couch as the airplane's fuselage, the coffee table as the plane's left wing, and pillows scattered on the floor as the injured passengers being treated by medical personnel. Use your imagination and your environment to tell the story: Paint a picture of who is at the scene and what is going on. Tell when the crash occurred, where the plane crashed, where the injured are, why officials think the plane went down, and how emergency rescue personnel are responding to and handling the crisis.

Write a news story that answers these questions and more. Then pick up a "microphone" (a marker or pen will do) and tell the story. When you are talking about the plane, point to the couch. When you are talking about the injured, refer to the "passengers" on the ground. If it is night, light a candle to simulate wreckage fire in the distance. The possibilities are endless. You may want to be alone while you are doing this at first so that you are free to take it seriously, or it may help to get classmates involved.

If you have several people participating, you can rotate roles and see how others might handle the situation. One person can be the reporter, one the fire chief, one a witness, and one the relative of a crash victim. In a case like this, the reporter has a lot to work with and many people to interview, and this practice will help sharpen not only the reporter's overall performance, but also his or her interview skills.

Be Open to Experiment

There are any number of ways to write and tell a story, so experiment. Find different ways of telling the same story. Try it without notes, as if you have just arrived on the scene. Use the environment to walk and talk the viewer through the story. If you make a mistake or forget what you were saying, find something in the environment to help get you back on track. This can be awkward at first, but over time you will notice an improvement in your ability to tell a story.

You need not be restricted to the living room or the classroom when practicing live. Go out to a forest preserve or other location outdoors. Bring a newspaper along. Look through the newspaper and find several stories. Find a hard news story, a feature story, a business story, a sports story, and a weather-related news story. Use the facts outlined in each story to create your live shot. Write a version of the story then present it. Here again, working with other members of your class may help add elements and reality to your presentations. It is important to take practice seriously, but have some fun with it as well.

When possible, use a video camera to record your practice sessions. The camera will record your strengths and weaknesses. It will also help you get comfortable standing in front of a camera and talking into the lens. If you are by yourself, set the camera on a tripod and lock it down. If you are with classmates or friends, take turns playing photojournalist to other reporters.

Watch Your Work

When you have completed your practice, sit down and take a look at the videotape. Almost immediately, you will find things that you would have or should have done differently. You will also discover a variety of things that may have exceeded your expectations. Herein lies the value of the exercise. It is important not only to see what you have done wrong, but to recognize what you have done right. You build success by focusing on the positive and recognizing the negative for what it is—not the other way around.

When you have finished watching your live news report, cue the tape up and do it again., This time, pay attention to those things you didn't like about your first presentation and either avoid them or correct the mistakes. Do it a third time as well. This is time consuming, but it is very good practice. Most successful reporters and anchors review their material on a regular basis and make corrections in their presentation or vocal delivery if they notice something they do not like.

When you have done the same story three or four times, go back and watch the takes back-to-back. There will likely be some very important and clear differences between the first take and the last one. You will be able to see if the changes you wanted to make were effective. You will also be able to see typical patterns you may follow. Some reporters and anchors, for example, have phrases or gestures they tend to repeat unconsciously; such unconscious repetitions become obvious when tapes are reviewed.

Whenever possible, you should have a professor or teacher look at your practice sessions as well. A knowledgeable person can be helpful in evaluating your performance and may recognize areas for improvement that you missed. Keep each session on a separate tape and mark each tape with the date and time of the practice session. You will be amazed by how much progress you can make in a relatively short period of time. It can be fun and encouraging to look old practice sessions to see how far you have come!

Watch Others' Work

It is also a good idea to watch and study the tapes of solid live newscasters. The best way to do this is to watch and record nightly newscasts. Look and listen carefully to those reporters you admire the most. Concentrate on how the reporter presents the story. The first time, watch the reporter and notice his or her mannerisms. Watch how he or she uses the face to help tell the story. Notice the gestures made by the reporter. Watch for any movement or referencing in the report. Ask yourself why the report is good. What is it about the style or look of the reporter that you admire?

If you have taped the report, replay it. This time, don't look at the reporter or the pictures. Close your eyes and listen to the report. Hear how the reporter has crafted his or her presentation. Listen to the transitions. Pay attention to the flow of the piece. Is it easy to listen to? Is it easy to understand? Can you picture what the report is showing based on what you hear from the reporter?

Watch and listen to a number of good live reporters. Learn their styles and learn to develop your own style. You don't want to mimic another reporter, but it never hurts to pick up a few good habits. It also helps to watch reporters who are not so good. It can be helpful to see what others are doing wrong. The goal is to avoid any behavior that will make you look or sound as if you don't know what you are doing. Remember, if you have credibility, you have everything. If you lack credibility, you have nothing.

Sample Practice Scenarios

The balance of this chapter is devoted to getting you started on practicing live television news reporting. I have created a number of scenarios and a list of related facts for each. Some of these examples are based on real news events; others are not. Your job is to craft a story and presentation for each case. Try to script a live report based on the information given, and use your surroundings to help support your report. Test your memory and organizational abilities by reviewing the facts of each case and presenting a report without writing anything down. Remember, you can do this alone or with the assistance of others.

In practicing, it is important to challenge yourself. Find different ways of telling the same story based on the facts. Practice with notes and without notes. Videotape your practice sessions whenever possible and review your work frequently. It would also be a good idea to work through each scenario several times. When you have completed all of them, go back and do each one again. Then look at the first and last versions of each story, comparing them and making notes.

Make sure you bring your taped practice sessions to a professor or teacher for review. It is also a good idea to review your material with peers. It is very important to learn how to take and use constructive criticism early on in your career. If you are too sensitive or too arrogant when it comes to the words of others, you will only hurt yourself in the long run.

Use the following scenarios and create your own as well. Newspapers, television news programs, and radio news reports are also great sources of material for practice. Remember, practice a variety of styles and cover a variety of material. Most live television news reporters are general assignment. This means they cover anything and everything that happens, from crime news to entertainment stories and everything in between!

Scene 1: Plane Crash

A Boeing 737 airplane took off from the local airport just before nine o'clock this morning. The plane was a vacation charter packed with people flying to Miami, Florida, for a cruise. Moments after taking off, something went catastrophically wrong. The plane banked to the right and knifed into the ground below. The crash site is right next to a heavily populated middle class housing subdivision. Parts of the plane have damaged some houses in the area, and there are some injuries on the ground.

Firefighters and rescue personnel from thirteen surrounding communities have been called into assist in fire fighting and search/rescue efforts. Part of the wreckage is in flames. Surprisingly, a good portion of the main cabin remains intact, and it looks as if several people may have survived the impact.

A number of residents from the nearby subdivision raced to the wreckage and are trying to provide assistance. Meanwhile, others are trying to help wounded neighbors who were hit by flying debris from the crash site.

One of the homes closest to the wreckage appears to have been struck by a piece of flaming material from the airplane. There is smoke and a small amount of flame coming from the roof of that home.

The plane went down in a field; it is very muddy and rain continues to fall. It will be very difficult for emergency personnel to get the necessary equipment to the scene. If survivors are found, they will likely have to be carried several hundred yards on stretchers to ambulances parked at the edge of the field.

There is some concern about the remainder of the fuel around the aircraft. The plane was fully loaded with fuel on takeoff. On impact, some of the fuel ignited, and some of it spilled but did not burn. However, the fire is spreading and is coming dangerously close to the balance of the fuel.

Scene 2: Bank Robbery

A bank robbery is under way at the First National Bank downtown. Three heavily armed men have taken over the bank and are holding more than a dozen people hostage. Police have set up barricades around the bank building and have closed down a number of streets leading to and from the bank. In addition, employees and customers have been evacuated from nearby businesses as a precaution.

The police chief held a news briefing. During the session, the chief revealed that the robbers had made a host of demands. The men are threatening to kill one or more of the hostages unless their demands are met. The chief would not go into specifics, but he did say that the robbers mean business. When asked about how police were alerted to the situation, the chief said a silent teller alarm had been triggered.

Police are in telephone contact with the leader of the robbers. All three men have bulletproof vests, high-powered weapons, and hundreds of rounds of ammunition. Police are calling for additional manpower. News choppers hover overhead.

A woman arrives on the scene in tears. You are able to talk with her. As it turns out, the woman is the wife of the bank manager who is inside. She tells you that her husband has a heart condition, and she is not sure if he has his medicine with him. She also mentions that this bank has been held up three times in the last six months.

A team of police snipers has arrived on the scene. They are taking up positions on the rooftops of nearby buildings. Since this is a bank robbery attempt, agents from the Federal Bureau of Investigations join in.

It is starting to get dark. All indications are that the bank robbers are getting edgy and impatient with authorities. With a hostage in front of him, one of the men peeks out the door and fires a shot up in the air to underscore that fact.

Scene 3: City Council Meeting

The city council is preparing to pass its new budget. The budget contains a number of items that have sparked controversy and debate in recent weeks. The ten million dollar operating plan contains increased funding for the police department and salary increases for council members. At the same time, funding for a number of social programs was cut back in order to balance the budget.

Those who would be impacted by the cuts are packing the council chambers. They are here to voice their anger and concern over the cuts and urge the council to reconsider. Their anger is compounded by the fact that the council is preparing to approve raises in salary at a time when even some council members admit that times are tight.

The mayor is defending the raises by pointing out that it has been more than a decade since the pay scale for council members has been adjusted. The mayor argues that you can't get good people to work for free in this day and age. The mayor says the raises are not much of a financial factor when you are talking about a ten million dollar spending plan.

The money being cut from some social service programs is being given to the police department. Crime is up 3 percent in the city this year. Violent crime is up nearly 15 percent. Gang activity and juvenile crime are also on the rise. The police chief says the new dollars will enable him to hire two new officers and buy several new squad cars. In addition, the increase will help fund education and awareness programs.

The council appears to be split on the issue of shifting funds from social services to law enforcement. The police department has received increases in funding in each of the past seven years, while social service funding has declined slowly but steadily over the same time period.

The debate will be lively. A number of the council members are up for reelection later this year; this may or may not have an impact on how they vote.

Scene 4: State Fair Opening

It is day one of the annual state fair. The week long event is expected to draw nearly a half million people to the fair grounds. This will be the largest fair in the ninety-five-year history of the event.

This year's event features livestock judging, a carnival, rides, games, food, and a series of display tents sponsored by local businesses. The entertainment this year is top-notch. Tonight, a popular rock and roll band from the 1980s takes the stage for two shows, and later this week the nation's number one country music band will roll into town for a concert here.

The fair is officially opened by the governor. Politicians

are out in force on day one, shaking hands, kissing babies, and passing out campaign literature. One of the main attractions each year is the rodeo. Riders from all over the country are in town to take part in the rodeo series that begins tonight. Tickets for this event have been sold out for weeks.

Security at this year's fair is much more visible than in previous years. Last year several people were arrested each night for fighting and drunkenness. This year there is another concern, gangs. Gang members have been hanging out in areas of the fair and are believed to be either selling or arranging for the sale of drugs. The fair has always been a family event, and the state police commissioner is vowing to keep it that way. Additional officers are working this year's event. Some are in uniform, while others are operating undercover.

Police are also keeping a close eye on the carnival games. In the past some of the games were rigged, and in previous years several operations were shut down for cheating fair goers with games that were impossible to win.

This is the last year for the state fair at this location. The fairgrounds property is going to be developed for other uses. The fair will continue at a new site which is being prepared across town.

Scene 5: Tornado Watch

A tornado watch has been issued for a portion of your viewing area. A watch means conditions are right for tornadic activity to develop. The winds are currently blowing at twenty miles per hour and gusting up to forty miles per hour. The sky is darkening and taking on a greenish tint. The temperature is dropping considerably. In the distance lightning is visible, and the rumble of thunder is clearly audible.

Radar shows the storm cell is gaining strength. The local disaster and emergency services office is beginning to receive telephone calls from people reporting significant wind damage. Weather spotters are out around the county watching the skies for signs of tornadic activity. Hail begins to fall in areas along the frontal edge of the storm system; the hail is pea sized in some cases but larger in others. The hail is causing damage to homes and cars.

A call comes in from a sheriff's deputy who has spotted what he believes to be a funnel cloud aloft. At that moment, the city's emergency sirens are sounded. Schoolchildren are quickly moved to the safe locations in their schools. Workers in office buildings are shuttled down into the basements. Those in their homes need to be reminded to find shelter on a lower level away from windows and other objects.

There is now confirmation that the funnel cloud has touched down and is in fact a tornado on the ground. The tornado is moving its way through an open field. It is miles away from the closest building and appears to pose no threat to the city or its residents. However, tornadoes are unpredictable and move quickly.

The fire department is called out to a blaze caused by a lightning strike to the roof of a home. No one has been injured in the fire, but high winds are making it difficult to control.

Radar shows another storm cell building behind the one currently moving through the area. This one looks as if it may become a severe weather threat as well.

Scene 6: Multi-vehicle Accident

A multi-vehicle accident has occurred on the city's main highway. It appears to be a chain reaction situation where two cars and a minivan ran into each other and were then hit by a truck. The accident is serious. Fire officials and rescue personnel are arriving on the scene. Police have blocked off all four lanes of the highway, bringing rush hour traffic to a dead stop.

It is evident that several people are trapped in one of the vehicles. Rescue workers bring out the jaws of life to try to free the victims. Firefighters work to secure the truck. It was not heavily damaged in the accident, but it does contain hazardous materials in fifty-gallon drums. It appears that one of the drums may have sprung a leak.

The minivan appears to have sustained the most damage. The vehicle was crushed between the cars and the truck. Rescue workers appear to have given up trying to save the driver. A van from the coroner's office has arrived on the scene. The front of the minivan is being covered with a tarp, and workers are coming in to remove the body.

Two victims have been removed from one of the cars. One of the victims is being placed in an ambulance for transport to a nearby hospital. The other sustained life threatening injuries and must be airlifted to a level one trauma center. Police have cleared an area for the emergency helicopter to land. The chopper sets down briefly. The victim is quickly placed in the helicopter and removed from the scene.

Several tow trucks arrive on the scene to help authorities separate and remove the vehicles. Car parts and glass cover a good portion of the road and will need to be cleared before the road can be reopened to traffic.

Traffic is backed up for miles in both directions, and many people are out of their vehicles watching workers at the scene.

Scene 7: Nursing Home Fire

A fire is burning on the third floor of a five-story nursing home facility. The blaze apparently began in one of the patient rooms on the third floor and is spreading quickly. There is somewhat of a panic as workers try to evacuate residents from all of the floors, including the one where the fire is located.

Firefighters arrive on the scene and immediately enter the building to take over rescue efforts. More than a dozen ambulances have been called in to take the evacuated patients to nearby hospitals. Some of the patients require treatment for smoke inhalation, others for injuries suffered during the evacuation. None of the injuries are life threatening.

The fire has spread upward to the fourth floor and is making rescue efforts very difficult. There are at least two residents and one staff member unaccounted for. The smoke on the floor where they were last seen is extremely dense, and firefighters are forced to feel their way around. The building's sprinkler system is only partially working and is doing little to retard the progress of the flames.

The scene has become quite chaotic on the outside. Flames and heavy smoke are visible. Relatives of the nursing home's patients and workers have arrived on the scene. They are visibly shaken and concerned about the welfare of their loved ones. People are crying and hugging each other. Many are questioning police as to the whereabouts of their relatives.

Additional fire assistance is called for. Several more engines arrive on the scene to support efforts. The fire chief is concerned about a storage room on the fourth floor that houses flammable chemicals and oxygen canisters. The fire is moving closer to the storage room, and all efforts now are focused on keeping the blaze away from it.

Meanwhile, little progress is being made on the third floor, where firefighters are desperately searching for the three missing people.

Scene 8: Search for Missing Children

The search is underway for two young boys who disappeared while on a canoe trip. The youngsters were last seen leaving a campsite and heading downriver in their small canoe. The boys were supposed to meet up with other group members at a site a mile away from the camp. The youngsters are now five hours late, and concern is growing among friends, family members, and park police.

Searchers set out in groups of four to try to retrace the path the youngsters may have taken. Some searchers return to the campsite where the boys were last seen. Others head downriver and begin the search for the canoe. The boys were wearing life vests when they left in the canoe.

Police are becoming concerned and suspicious. These boys are good kids and are very knowledgeable about canoeing. Relatives say they are also not the kind of kids to go out exploring on their own. At this point, officials at the scene consider all the options: the kids are still in the boat and are lost; something went wrong and they ended up separated from the boat and are in the water or on the banks somewhere; or they met with foul play.

A helicopter is called in to aid in the search. The chopper flies back and forth over the river area searching the water and the banks for signs of the kids and/or the canoe. Search dogs are being used to try to track the youngsters on the ground. The weather is relatively calm, and the temperature is warm; but it is getting dark, and the temperature is expected to fall considerably after sunset. The boys are without food, and the only water available is river water.

Searchers combing the banks of the river have found something. A canoe paddle very similar to the one the boys were using has been found in the water a few feet from shore. The paddle is fished out of the water and checked for identification markings. The leader of the canoe trip notices a number on the paddle handle. That number is checked against the group equipment list, and the paddle is the one that was assigned to the boys.

Scene 9: Snowstorm

One of the heaviest snowstorms in city history is underway. So far nearly nine inches of snow have fallen, and the forecast predicts that another two to three inches will fall before it is all over. The large snowfall is wreaking havoc with just about everything you can imagine.

On the roadways, many motorists are stranded and waiting for help. Police and tow trucks, however, are having a hard time getting to people because of road conditions.

There are a number of minor accidents on major arteries that are making the traffic situation even worse. Snow plows and salt trucks are out in force, but they just can't seem to clear the snow away fast enough.

On the railways, trains are at a halt in most cases. Rail crews are having similar problems trying to clear tracks and keep trains moving. Some trains are stuck in the station, while others are sitting still on the tracks. Commuter and freight traffic has been slowed to a virtual standstill.

At the airport there is a ground stop, and no planes are taking off or landing. Some passengers stranded at the terminal building will be able to find hotel rooms, but others will have to sleep on cots at the airport. The closure of the airport is causing problems nationwide. Planes and crew needed at other airports are stuck here, and passengers looking to connect through your city can't get in or out.

The mayor is calling on all residents to stay at home if at all possible. It is not a state of emergency, but there is a growing concern. All snow removal personnel are now on twenty-four-hour shifts and won't get a real break until the situation has settled.

Making matters worse, the heavy snow has brought down tree branches which have, in turn, brought down some power lines. Thousands of people are now without electricity—which means they are without heat in many cases. The snow continues to fall.

Scene 10: Execution Protest

A convicted killer is scheduled to die by lethal injection at one minute after midnight. The man has been on death row for more than a decade for the murder of a city police officer. The man's conviction has been upheld by both the state supreme court and the U.S. Supreme Court. The only one that can stop the execution is the governor.

Dozens of people are protesting outside the prison where the execution is scheduled to take place. Many of the protesters are activists who oppose the death penalty. Others are supporters of the condemned man who believe he is innocent. Furthermore, there is some evidence to support the idea that the man on death row is not responsible for the death of the police officer.

The protesters are met by another group. This group includes many police officers and friends and family members of the slain officer. They have come to see justice served in this case. There are loud and emotional exchanges between some members of the groups. They are physically kept apart by members of the state police.

A department of corrections spokesman comes out to update the press on the condition of the condemned inmate on this last day. He has ordered his last meal. He has asked for a steak, potato, beans, and blueberry pie. The spokesman says the condemned man's mother is visiting with him now and that his priest is also with him.

The governor is usually quick to decline any last minute or last second appeals by or on the behalf of an inmate. However, in this case, there are some concerns about the conviction. While the conviction has been upheld by all courts of appeal, some witnesses have admitted that they lied at the man's trial. Supporters say those admissions should be enough to halt the execution. However, prosecutors say the conviction in this case could stand even if the witness accounts were eliminated from the matter altogether.

The governor is reviewing the case and consulting with his legal experts. It is now 11:30 PM, only half an hour before the execution will be carried out.

Scene 11: Fireworks Display

The city is preparing to put on one of the biggest Fourth of July fireworks celebrations in the nation. More than a million people are expected to flock to the lakefront to take in the magnificent display. The city is spending nearly a hundred thousand dollars on the fireworks extravaganza. The fireworks will be set off in concert with the local symphony orchestra and its rendition of the *William Tell Overture*. The actual show will last only about twenty-five minutes, but it will be one of the loudest and most colorful ever put on.

The annual fireworks show is a family tradition for many. It is an all-day affair. The show itself starts at half past nine in the evening, but people begin flocking to the lake front as early as seven o'clock in the morning to stake out a prime piece of real estate. This is also one of the year's largest outdoor cooking events. Just about everyone brings a charcoal or mini–propane grill. There are even cooking contests for specialty foods such as ribs.

People bring blankets and chairs with them. A few people even bring tents to nap in or to escape from the sun for a while. The harbor is filled with hundreds of boats, and the boats are filled with hundreds of people who will party and take in the fireworks on the water. Several of the taller buildings in town are hosting rooftop parties.

With so many people packed in to see the show, safety is the number one priority. Last year, a few dozen people were arrested for creating problems at the celebration, and extra police are out patrolling the area around the lakefront and in nearby parks. Furthermore, the fire department is inspecting the barges out on the lake from which the fireworks will be launched. Although the pyrotechnics company has been working on this show for months, even with careful preparation things can go wrong. Last year a shell fired off but never left the ground. That shell set off others and led to a ground explosion which killed one worker.

This year the city has worked to ensure the show is more spectacular and safer than ever.

Scene 12: Train Derailment

A freight train moving through the city has derailed. The derailment occurred at a crossing near a heavily populated section of town. A problem with the track at that grade crossing sent more than ten railroad cars off the tracks. At least two of the cars are tankers carrying dangerous materials, and three of the cars are carrying coal. The other five are boxcars carrying a variety of things.

The immediate threat comes from the tanker cars leaking hazardous materials. A white cloud of gas begins to rise from one of the tankers. The chemical cloud prompts fire officials to begin evacuating residents from nearby homes, offices, and schools. Police close off several streets leading to and from the scene of the derailment. The fire department is working with the railroad to determine exactly what chemicals it is dealing with.

All traffic on the rail has come to a complete halt and will remain at a stop until the wreckage can be cleared and the track can be repaired. This, of course, will have a huge impact on thousands of commuters and on freight shipments through the area.

Several firefighters report respiratory problems and are transported to a local hospital for treatment and observation. Additional hazardous material handlers are called to the scene to help contain the spill and transfer the balance of the unspilled chemical into a truck tanker for removal from the scene. There is an effort to minimize ground exposure to the chemical for fear of water contamination.

The chemical spill is top priority, but the coal spill is also a concern. Tens of thousands of pounds of coal sit in the middle of the street. The coal piles are blocking the most direct route to the tanker cars. Workers must clear a path through the coal without exposing themselves to chemical fumes. The railroad is moving special equipment into the area which will be used to upright the cars and place them back on the tracks once the spill is contained.

Scene 13: World Series

The first game of the World Series will be played tonight at your team's stadium. This is the first time in modern history that your ball club has made it to the Series. The city is going wild over its team. Fans are flocking to the stadium early to take pictures and buy all of the souvenirs they can handle. There are only forty-five thousand seats in the stadium. All of the tickets were sold weeks in advance, but there are thousands of people still trying to get in.

The face value of the average ticket is seventy dollars. However, there are scalpers around the stadium selling these tickets for upwards of a thousand dollars each. Police are out in force trying to keep the scalpers away, but that is difficult since the demand for seats is so high.

Police are also on the lookout for others trying to make a quick buck off of the team's success. Officials have seized tens of thousands of dollars worth of stolen or unlicensed material from street vendors. Police have confiscated everything from hats and pins to bats and balls, and several people have been arrested for selling the items.

Tailgating is usually reserved for football games, but many fans who can't get into the stadium have set up outside. Some have brought portable TVs and radios. Many more have grills, burgers, brats, and beer ready for game time. Hundreds of fans have illegally parked themselves in the stadium lot, but police seem to be a bit too busy to notice. There are already some drunk fans who are letting everyone know in slurred and uncertain terms why their team is the best.

Fans of the opposing team are arriving as well. There are spirited discussions between fans of the two teams about why one team is better than the other. The discussions get very loud but never escalate beyond a war of words. It is easy to sense that fans on both sides recognize that this is a moment in sports history. The president of the United States has also arrived in town, and his motorcade is working its way to the stadium, where he will toss out the first pitch.

Scene 14: Teachers' Strike

Teachers in the city's largest school district have announced they are going on strike to protest the lack of progress in contract negotiations with the school board. Teachers have been in the classroom for months without a contract. The teachers' union says the two sides have reached an impasse. The school board says the union is making demands but will not consider concessions.

Teachers want a three-year contract with a 12 percent pay increase over the life of the pact. The union is also seeking expanded pension benefits and wants to iron out job security issues tied to the use of longer-term substitute teachers.

The school board is offering a three-year contract with a guaranteed 8 percent pay increase over the life of the agreement. The board wants more control over the pension plan because it feels it will be better able to manage and increase the funds. The board does not want any restrictions on its use of longer-term substitute teachers.

The strike will impact about ten thousand students from grade school through high school. The board says it will seek to replace striking teachers and keep classes going. But the union and many parents are critical of that plan. The strike threatens to block the senior class from completing graduation requirements and may force many seniors to attend summer school sessions.

Seniors aside, most students do not seem to be concerned about the situation. Many like the idea of the mini-vacation a strike would present if the board can't replace teachers. Parents, on the other hand, are angry with both sides and are letting them know it in no uncertain terms. A parents' group has taken out an ad in the local newspaper urging both sides to settle this matter because it is the children who are being caught in the middle.

No new bargaining sessions have been scheduled.

7

The "Real World": Internships

Getting started in the "real world" of live television news reporting almost always means an internship at a commercial television news operation. In fact, important research suggests that an internship is among the most important steps in landing a job in this field. Consider the following study by Vernon Stone, journalism professor emeritus at the highly respected University of Missouri–Columbia.

Internships in TV and Radio News: Paid and Unpaid

Interns are everywhere and usually without pay. ... Hundreds of interns take home [no pay] for working ten to forty hours a week in television and radio newsrooms. In lieu of money, most are "paid" in college credits and real-life experience that is unavailable on their campuses. They gain an edge in the extreme competition for regular paying jobs.

Sounds like something every student would want? Most do, and that brings a downside. Students by the thousands now seek internships, and stations say they can meet the demand only by offering them without pay. If stations follow federal

137

regulations, interns get diluted experience—they are severely restricted in the work they are allowed to do. Paid internships are worth more professionally as well as financially, but are available to few of the many students who may want them. This report looks at the value of internships, how unpaid have crowded out paid internships, rules and goals for stations, and the question of too few paid [interns].

Pipelines to Payrolls

Internships pay off at hiring time. Interns are favored applicants in the growing competition for jobs. In both television and radio, former interns at the same station account for at least one of every six hires. My 1991 survey found that for every three TV interns on duty during a twelve-month period, one who had served there before was being hired. In radio, former interns, known quantities, accounted for well over half of all hires.

If it doesn't happen by graduation day, maybe later. You may have excelled as an intern, but there is no opening. Or, especially if you interned at a major-market station, you may need to get experience in a smaller market first. But do a good job as an intern and they remember.

Further evidence that internships are pipelines to payrolls comes from my 1990–91 Freedom Forum–sponsored survey of journalists. As [Table 7.1] shows, half of the broadcast news people working in the 1990s—three in five for TV and two in five for radio news—are former interns. And time after time in the careers survey, [journalists] said interning was one of their most valuable college experiences.

The women of broadcast news are more likely than the

Table 7.1. Journalists Who Have Held Internships

	Unpaid Only (%)	Paid Only (%)	Paid & Unpaid (%)	None (%)	N
All TV	37.6	10.8	8.8	43.1	1,781
Men	32.2	10.2	7.5	50.1	1,142
Women	47.2	11.7	11.2	29.9	632
Whites	38.1	11.0	8.0	42.9	1,565
Minorities	33.2	8.9	15.3	42.6	202
All Radio	27.1	10.1	4.8	58.0	414
Men	22.8	9.7	3.3	64.2	268
Women	34.9	11.0	7.5	46.6	146
Whites	26.6	9.4	4.9	59.1	384
Minorities	33.3	22.2	3.7	40.8	27

men to have served as interns. That's explained partially by the finding that the women average several years younger than the men. Internships had become more prevalent by the time women went to college.

Minorities in TV have served internships at about the same rate as others. Though a number of stations have paid internships that are earmarked for their use, minority journalists are only slightly more likely than others to have served a paid internship. In radio, minorities are ex-interns more often than others, and the edge comes in paid internships.

Unpaid internships sometimes lead to paid ones. Roughly half of the 20 percent of TV journalists who have held paid internships have also served on an unpaid basis. Some stations have both kinds of internships, and a student can be promoted from unpaid one term to paid the next.

Unpaid Internships Take Over

Time was when many journalism schools recognized only paid internships, and the majority of TV and radio stations that offered internships paid students for their work. At the University of Wisconsin–Madison in the early 1970s, we granted journalism credit for internships only through a seminar. ... A paid internship was a prerequisite for the seminar. We reasoned that anyone can work free. The few students we were ready to recommend for internships had too much to offer to give their work away. They had taken rigorous courses in news writing, basic reporting, and camera-reporting. With minimal breaking in, they were ready to do work that justified pay. They did so, and newsrooms were happy with them year after year.

But then television journalism became very popular. Communication enrollments grew. Young men and women knocked on newsroom doors, willing to work for free to get a start. Stations came under pressure from universities to provide internships to most students who wanted them. Stations could not put them all on payrolls. So unpaid internships came into their own, and found takers. Selectivity became a casualty, elitism a dirty word. By the early 1980s, the Wisconsin seminar had to recognize unpaid internships.

To see what happened, let's compare national surveys I conducted fifteen years apart [Table 7.2]. Unpaid internships, once rolling, tended to crowd the paid ones off the road. In 1976, 57 percent of the TV and 81 percent of the radio stations with interns paid at least some of them. By 1991, only 21 percent of the TV and 32 percent of radio stations with interns were paying.

Counting interns instead of stations, 45 percent of the [interns] in TV news were paid in 1976, but that had dropped to 10 percent by 1991. In radio, 80 percent of all interns were paid in 1976, but only 21 percent in 1991. In both years, radio was less likely than television to have news interns of any kind.

Academic credit was awarded for internships served at 84 percent of the TV and 66 percent of the radio stations in 1976. The 1991 survey did not ask that, but one would expect an even higher percentage. The growing use of unpaid interns goes with compensating in college credits instead of money.

Table 7.2. Newsrooms' Changing Use of Interns

	Television		Radio	
	Paid	Unpaid	Paid	Unpaid
Using Interns				
1976	27.4%	25.4%	18.6%	4.4%
1991	17.7%	76.5%	8.2%	17.6%
Average Interns per Term in Newsrooms with Interns				
*1976	1.5	2.0	1.2	1.3
1991	1.9	4.0	1.4	1.7
Estimated Summer Number				
1976	260	315	1,200	310
1991	260	2,320	670	1,735
Estimated Total Interns				
1976	520	630	2,400	620
1991	520	4,640	1,340	3,470
Est. Full-Time Work Force				
1976		9,000		12,000
1991		20,400		10,500

* Not surveyed in 1976, but adapted from 1991 values.

Growing Numbers

A light shower turned into a downpour. In fifteen years, the number of interns quadrupled in TV and went up by half again in radio news, far outpacing the workforce change in both media. Many more radio and TV stations offered internships in the 1990s than in the 1970s. The number of TV newsrooms using summer interns went up from 48 percent in 1976 to 85 percent in 1991. Radio stayed at 25 percent. Many new stations went on the air during the fifteen years, too. News operations increased from about 625 to 750 in television, and from 5,400 to 5,800 in commercial radio.

Paid internships are still out there. Indeed, TV news had as many in 1991 as in 1976. Surprised? I was when I multiplied the averages by the stations with interns and came up with the same projected 260 paid interns for each year. (This comes from there being more stations in 1991 and more interns per station.) Radio, on the other hand, cut its paid interns by almost half. But it's unpaid interns who exploded the totals. Seven times as many were in TV newsrooms in 1991 as in 1976. Radio's increases were fivefold.

Though the 1991 survey asked about only summer interns, [Table 7.2] gives estimates for total interns. Here's how. The 1976 survey found that roughly as many stations used interns during the regular academic year as in summer. Educators and industry leaders indicate that is still the case. We also know that turnover takes place each term, but that many students serve more than one term. The rough estimates of twelve-month totals for 1991 come from letting repeaters cancel out term turnover, ... thus multiplying summer values by two terms instead of three. (If you prefer another multiple, plug it in.)

Now, think for a moment about those totals—roughly five thousand students interning in TV newsrooms and five thousand in radio every year. Compared to eleven hundred in TV and three thousand in radio back in the mid-1970s. In the summer months and probably during the academic year, that is one intern for every eight regular full-time news employees in television and one for every four in radio. Interns everywhere you turn. Newsrooms have had to add work stations. And while they have not often let interns increase payrolls, stations have absorbed costs in the form of supervisory time and overhead. Facilities don't come free.

TV newsrooms with unpaid interns typically have three or four. But a third have five or more. In the twenty-five largest markets, two-thirds have five or more and nearly a fourth have ten or more—up to twenty-five—unpaid interns at a time. You need a classroom just to sit them down together. Some newsrooms even have assistant or associate news directors primarily to supervise interns. They're de facto faculty for universities.

Again, that grand total—roughly ten thousand students a year are working as interns and hoping to get regular jobs in broadcast journalism. Such a number suggests that supply exceeds demand. It does. Surveys I did in the mid-1980s showed that broadcast news job applicants outnumbered entry-level jobs by at least two to one. [See Vernon A. Stone, "Broadcasting Market Flooded by Non-News Radio-TV Majors," *Journalism Educator* 42 (Spring 1987):20-23.]

It became even more competitive. In 1988, TV news directors said in my survey that they received about sixty applications for every entry-level opening they filled. The ratio was twenty-four to one. Since the same person may apply to many stations, these are the ratios of applications to hires, not of applicants to hires.

But by the early 1990s, joint Missouri and Ohio State studies showed that the supply of graduates in broadcast journalism and more general broadcasting and telecommunications totaled about ten times as many as the entry-level jobs available. Many of the graduates did not apply for broadcast jobs, of course, but a major oversupply is still indicated. (See Lee B. Becker, Vernon A. Stone and Joseph D. Graf, "Entry-Level Pay in Broadcast News: Is Oversupply an Explanation for Low Wages?" paper presented at the annual convention of the Association for Education in Journalism and Mass Communication in Atlanta, in August 1994.)

Playing by the Rules

For the station, paying or not paying makes a big difference. If paid, the intern is on the payroll and can work pretty much as regular staff, with all appropriate benefits and obligations. If unpaid, the intern must not be treated like regular staff or even an employee trainee. Else, the Fair Labor Standards Act (FLSA) requirements on minimum wage, overtime pay, etc. apply. To be exempt from FLSA rules governing an "employee," the unpaid student intern must meet *all* of the following criteria:

1. The training, even though it includes actual operation of the facilities of the employer, is similar to that which would be given in a vocational school.
2. The training is for the benefit of the trainees or students.
3. The trainees do not displace regular employees but work under their close observation.

4. The employer that provides the training derives no immediate advantage from the activities of the trainees or students; and on an occasion the employer's operations may actually be impeded.
5. The trainees or students are not necessarily entitled to a job at the conclusion of the training period.
6. The employer and the trainees or students understand that they are not entitled to wages for the time spent training.

Those criteria are detailed in the U.S. Department of Labor's "Employment Relationship Under the Fair Labor Standards Act" (WH Publication 1297) quoted in J. Laurent Scharff, "Structuring Student Internships to Avoid Problems," *Legal Notes* distributed to RTNDA [Radio-Television News Directors Association] members in October 1992.

While not necessary, formal college course credit for the internship can be seen as evidence that it's for the benefit of the student and that the intern is not being treated as an employee. The provisions here have been interpreted to mean that an intern should not be given work that might displace the work of a regular employee or otherwise benefit the employer.

If a station strictly meets the six FSLA criteria, an unpaid intern may tend to be little more than an observer or "gofer" (as in "go for" coffee) or "extra" doing things the newsroom could do without ("employer ... derives no immediate advantage"). That's a far cry from the old paid internships at WTMJ TV and Radio, Milwaukee, where University of Wisconsin journalism students wrote, edited, reported, and even went on air. Unpaid interns no doubt still do these things in many of the stations without union employees, as is the case for most small

and middle markets. Some of these stations get by with violat-
ing wage and hour laws for regular staff—so why not interns?
But in major markets, unionized staff serve as watchdogs to
protect their jobs from free labor, often leaving only a watered
down experience for the unpaid intern.

Win-Win as a Goal

Helping in even a small way to get things done professionally in a major-market newsroom may be worth more than
poorly supervised hands-on work in a bush league shop. At
least that is the thinking of Tony Villasana, news operations director at KSDK-TV, St. Louis. One of his duties is to oversee
an internship program that about four hundred students have
completed since 1983. The interns are unpaid and must earn
academic credit. As Villasana sees it:

> The time each intern spends with us is a win-win situa-
> tion for the student and the station. The intern is given
> the opportunity to learn from media professionals in a
> setting that is unavailable in many colleges and universi-
> ties. The station, on the other hand, benefits from those
> services the intern performs. For example, even an-
> swering the phone at the assignment desk gives the in-
> tern the experience of taking calls that might lead to a
> story. He or she learns what is potentially newsworthy
> and how to determine priorities and react accordingly.
> Interns who do an outstanding job are often referred to
> news departments seeking entry-level producers, re-
> porters, etc. Interns whose performance is mediocre or
> marginal quickly learn that their chances of competing

are not good. While it may be a bitter pill to swallow, it's an important one in deciding on a career.

The Television Sore Thumb

Valuable as unpaid internships may be, students working their way through school may not be able to make the financial sacrifice. And television stands out among the mass media as the one least likely to pay interns. Radio is a close second from last. Newspapers do best.

In a 1990–91 survey of 1990 journalism and mass communication graduates, Professor Lee Becker of Ohio State asked those who had been interns whether they were paid. By media, how many of those internships carried pay?

1. Daily newspapers, 64 percent
2. Public relations, 48 percent
3. Advertising, 45 percent
4. Magazines, 45 percent
5. Radio, 25 percent
6. Television, 20 percent

The percentages shown in [Table 7.2] from my 1991 TV and radio surveys differed slightly from Becker's. Our surveys differed in that I surveyed news directors regarding all interns, whereas Becker surveyed communication graduates only. His figures or mine, it matters little—TV and radio news are not in the same ballpark with daily newspapers. (Source: Lee B. Becker, "Survey of Journalism and Mass Communication Graduates 1990." Summary Report, School of Journalism, Ohio State University, June 1991.)

Why are TV and Radio news so far behind everyone else? Worse off financially? Not television. Across three decades, my surveys have shown that commercial TV stations' newsrooms are profitable, even in small markets. Daily newspapers, magazines and radio stations fall to competition and go out of business. But network affiliated TV stations almost never fold—they're too busy making money. Yet their internships carry pay even less often than the ones in radio, where just staying in business is challenging for many stations.

More inclined to exploration? Maybe. Many stations pay news staff less than they would make in other media. Clearly less than TV stations can afford. But other media have their robber barons, too. So that may or may not be the major factor.

Supply and demand? Too many would-be broadcast journalists? Yes. That appears to be the best explanation—the oversupply of students who want internships. Of course students want them. Half the people working in broadcast news today had them. They're tickets to jobs. So faculty and students come begging and stations hate to say no. Besides, it has long been found that many news directors welcome opportunities to contribute to the education of their future fellow professionals. At least as long ago as my "Broadcast News Educators and the Profession," *Journalism Quarterly* 47 (Spring 1970): 162–165.

Reassesment in Order

Greater use of paid internships for TV and radio news was suggested by the Roper Organization in reporting its 1987 survey of broadcast executives on the topic of higher education and career preparation. The *Electronic Media Career Preparation Study,* commissioned and distributed by RTNDA, concluded (pages 51–52):

> Internship programs, as they are currently organized, are not providing students with the types of experience which executives feel they need ... One of the reasons for this may be that the overwhelming percentage of executives whose stations offer internships say these internships are unpaid ... Given the large number of college students today who pay for their schooling through a combination of direct aid and work-study programs or other jobs outside of school, it may be that students cannot realistically afford to take advantage of unpaid internship programs. This may be an area where the broadcast industry might have to reassess its own policies and procedures and make certain changes in order to achieve its objectives.

Reassessment is also in order for higher education. The academy bears at least as much responsibility as the industry, particularly for the surplus of students trying to get into the field. Faced with student numbers and limited campus facilities, educators have turned over a significant part of broadcast news education to the industry.

Leading educators are among those who have suggested that exploitation may be involved in internships that pay in academic credit instead of money and that "the academic unit is at least an accomplice in this exploitative system." So wrote Trinity University Professors Robert O. Blanchard and William

G. Christ in their book *Media Education and the Liberal Arts: A Blueprint for the New Professionalism* (Hillsdale, N.J.: Lawrence Erlbaum Associates, 1993), pp. 115–118.

That may well be, but when working TV and radio journalists are in effect teaching hundreds of hours of course credits, for which faculty are paid, who is exploiting whom?

More paid internships are to be encouraged for accomplished students who can do a professional job that justifies wages. But at least half of the five thousand or so who are now in newsrooms probably have not reached that point in their development. For them, unpaid internships can make sense. These interns may make a financial sacrifice, as indeed they do to earn their college credits.

In return many if not most gain a priceless opportunity to see broadcast journalism up close, to contribute what they can to real-life news operations, and perhaps to make career decisions. Such benefits may be worth far more than a few weeks or months on a minimum wage payroll. That internship, unpaid though it may be, looks good on a [resume] at job-hunting time.

Reprinted with permission of Bonus Books, Inc., 160 E. Illinois St., Chicago, IL 60611. *Let's Talk Pay in Television and Radio News,* Chapter 9, Vernon Stone, 1993. Reproduced by permission of the publisher via Copyright Clearance Center, Inc.

Making the Most of Internships
Get on Air

Stone's research shows that internships are becoming the rule in television news, but what rules should you follow when looking to land one? There are several schools of thought. News directors who hire and in many cases coordinate intern programs are among the best sources for straightforward advice. Chicago television news director Jim Disch explains some of the important questions and concerns with respect to getting a successful start.

> Your first job is to find a place that will let you on the air. This is not whimsical advice. I know too many people that are pretty good and have the vision of getting their foot in the door. By that they mean landing a job at a station in a major market. You certainly can land jobs in major markets as production assistants, as desk assistants, and the temptation to do this can be great because you are thinking "Okay, I'm now working at this big TV station, I am not getting paid much if anything, I don't have much responsibility, but when something comes up—bingo! I'm going to move right into it." The truth of the matter it almost never happens this way. Maybe once in a thousand cases. I'll give you an example. Over and over again, when a reporter position opens in this city, there are real good reporters here. The problem for interns is that they will never get a chance to go out and report. When the job opening comes, we are also getting tapes from people who have been out there for five, six, seven years or god knows how long doing a dozen live shots a week. Who do you think is going to have a better tape? A better chance? It is a slam dunk, the person who has been out there doing it.

Choose the Right Market

If you really want to be a live television news reporter and make the most of your internship opportunity, you may want to take a serious look at medium- or small-market stations. Look for a station that will let you on the air to prove and improve your skills. Don't try to back into it, and avoid trying to get your foot in the door. Starting out small is oftentimes the best route to making it big.

After spending several months at a small- or medium-market station where you are actually doing the work, you will be able to build that important "escape tape" (resume tape). It is this tape that will help you move up or move on to the next station.

Young reporters tend to focus entirely too much on market size. Maybe it is because in school we learn that the big dollars are in the big markets. The glamour and excitement are reserved for New York, Los Angeles, or Chicago. This is part of the problem. You should be less concerned with the size of the market and more concerned with the quality of the news operation you will be going to.

If, for example, you are offered an opportunity in market number 53—should you go? The question you should be asking yourself and your internship advisor is, "What do we know about the station and its reputation for news and opportunity?" Let's say this station in [market 53] does one newscast a day. The show is your standard half hour variety. In terms of resources, the station has one live truck and a staff of a half dozen reporters. In this case, you will be lucky to ever get a live shot.

Now let's go to market number 110. Here you are offered a chance at a small family-owned station. It is a station that takes news seriously, and one in which the owners have invested a lot in technology and staff. This station wants to make the most of its local origin program dollars so it produces about four hours of news a day. Here you are likely to be doing a lot of work, a lot of live. Here you will be getting the experience and building your tape for the next move. Yes, it is fifty-seven markets smaller in terms of population—but it is much larger for you in your quest for experience.

In small to medium markets, you also get a chance to get better. Many of these stations will give you the day in, day out practice you need. You will also be working with reporters and anchors of very different skill levels. It is from these coworkers that you will begin to establish the measuring stick for your success. You will learn a lot about writing and presentation from those who are very good at both. You will also learn from the mistakes of others. There is no substitute for the knowledge you can gain from working under someone whose work is superior to yours. That individual can help guide you and teach you what you need to learn to reach his or her level.

This is actually a very exciting time for television reporters just graduating or looking to land a productive internship, as Northwestern University professor Patricia Dean explains.

> Things have changed so much over the past ten years in this business. First of all, early on the cost of technology meant that live shots were reserved for the middle and large markets, not the markets most reporters started in at the time. This meant that you didn't get live shots until the second or third station you ended up at. Now we have a situation where students who intern at small stations will likely end up

doing live shots. That is incredible to me. The first time I heard about students that were still learning, thrown live on the air, I was astounded. It is almost a nonissue these days. We assume that you will likely end up live, and all of the students know this now. It used to be that no matter what the station, only certain reporters got on the air live. There were not that many live trucks. Now everyone has live trucks, and more of them. At one time, only breaking stories were live, now every other type of story is live as well.

Take Charge

As Stone pointed out in his research, the internship is often the "pipeline to the payroll." A successful internship will help you land a job at the station you are an intern for or at another station that admires the work you did during your internship. In either case, it is a resume tape of your work that will open up the doors for you. A resume tape contains your best work. It shows news directors where you are at in terms of writing and live presentation and what potential you have.

This is an extremely competitive field. Job applicants far outnumber the positions available—and the big jobs in big markets are among the hardest to land, even with a wealth of experience and talent. The level of competition is no less among interns. It is for this reason that you must be tenacious and unrelenting. A career in this field is a sacrifice from the beginning. Pay will be low or nonexistent. Interns often work weekends and holidays. The hours can be early morning or late at night, rarely does any journalist land a nine-to-five gig. You must show your bosses that you are not only talented and capable, but also tough and willing to learn.

As an intern, take every opportunity given to you and learn to create your own. Sitting back and waiting for things to be handed to you is the wrong way to get started in this business. Come in every day with story ideas, things that you have researched and would like to pursue. Realize that you will likely not get an opportunity to do a quarter of what you ask to do, but you will get opportunity if you show your interest.

Some news directors have no intention of letting interns on the air. However, those same news directors may do so if the intern presses for a chance. You don't want to aggravate the news director or anyone else, but you do want to let them know that the only one you will get coffee for is yourself. Be persistent.

Be patient as well. Often, your big chance to get out in the field comes when something happens to another reporter. A number of interns started their careers filling in for reporters who called in sick or went on vacation or were unable to report for one reason or another. These are the times where the news director will say, "Okay, you've been looking for your chance, here it is." Take the bull by the horns. Remember the three Ps of being a good intern. Persistence, Patience, Preparedness.

Try More Than One

You may find that one internship does not provide the level of experience you need. Or that the type of internship you have selected isn't ideal. You might have enough time for multiple internships. Professor Dean points out that such experience can be extremely valuable.

I am one of those that advises to get as many internships as possible. First of all, it gives you a touch of the real world. Nothing is more eye opening, and you ought to know what is going on and what you are getting into. At universities we certainly try to teach real-world concepts. The reality is though, that learning what it is like to be in a real newsroom is something you must experience. You will either love it or hate it. You can learn so much if given an opportunity to do more than get coffee and answer phones. The first internship, anything you get is great. Just getting into a real newsroom and getting exposed to the news environment is important. After that, try to get into that shop where someone will let you do something. If you write well enough, they might use a script, they might just let you go out in the field. The other thing that happens is that you are sitting around and that big story breaks and no one else is around—you get to really do the work you want to do. There is really no substitute for the internship. It is crucial in journalism.

8

Sensitivity

Importance of Sensitivity

As a live television news reporter, you will be placed in a
host of uncomfortable and sometimes traumatic settings.
These can be difficult for you to deal with as a person and
as a professional and may make your live performance that
much more challenging. What many reporters fail to consider is the impact the scene is having on victims, witnesses,
and others who will be around long after the lights have
dimmed and the live trucks have left. Many reporters coming right out of colleges and universities have not been
taught that a major component of journalism is sensitivity.
The truth of the matter is that sensitivity should be right up
there with the who, what, when. where, why, and how. I
have often believed that "Sensitivity 101" should be among
the graduation requirements for reporters.

It is important to understand that no matter how sensitive you think you are or how sensitive you believe your station is, perception is reality. If people who are watching
your station think the presentation is insensitive—it is. You
may very well be a sensitive reporter. You may not, how-

ever, be aware that some of what you are saying is offensive to a certain segment of your audience.

In a newsroom environment, insensitive remarks or scripting can be filtered out by producers, executive producers, or other news managers. This is not always true with live field reports. Live reporting is fluid and often involves a reporter ad-libbing a portion of the report. Unfortunately, this sometimes means a reporter is not paying attention to every word, phrase, or thought he or she utters, and may not be thinking about how what is said may be interpreted. Under these less controlled circumstances, it is a lot easier to make a comment that is perceived as insensitive.

Many news organizations are doing a lot of self-evaluation these days when it comes to sensitivity and their product. One of the better ideas to come from such work is the creation of internal sensitivity committees. Committees like these meet on a regular basis and discuss the content of and approaches to news coverage. These committees generally include members of the news staff, the sales staff, and the administration. Their input and diversity help news operations develop and implement policies and strategies for dealing with sensitivity concerns.

Special Concerns

Sensitivity is a multifaceted issue that covers all aspects of news reporting. The main areas of concern center around the presentation, the subject matter, and the viewership. Recent studies have shown that people find the news media insensitive in its overall approach to reporting news. The grade is even worse when it comes to the coverage of crime, accident, and death stories. These stories also represent the lion's share of live breaking news coverage opportunities. In light of such dismal public opinion, it is critical for the live news reporter to be much more conscious of what he or she is saying and of what video images are chosen to support the story.

Flexible Standards

There are standards that govern what can and can't be aired on television. There are no standards, however, that deal with what should or should not be aired. What may make air in Los Angeles or Chicago may not play in Peoria. Certain markets tend to approach the coverage of news much differently that others. Many are very conservative with respect to what may appear in a news story, others are more liberal in their presentation of pictures and subject matter. A more conservative station may show a body bag being removed from the scene of a shooting. A less conservative station may show a shot of the body on the ground before it is bagged. This can be true as well at different stations in the same market. Two of the three network affiliates may maintain a conservative news policy—the third may go out of its way to be different. The first challenge to you as a live reporter is to know very clearly what is expected of you and what is an appropriate approach to your story based on the news philosophy adopted by your organization. Let's begin with the pictures.

Scene: You arrive at the scene of a bank robbery. There are several gunmen holding hostages. Police have surrounded the bank, their weapons are drawn. Two of the gunmen exit the bank and begin shooting at the police officers. Police begin to fire back at the gunmen. Several officers and hostages are hit by gunfire. The suspects are finally killed by police snipers. Your photographer has captured all of this on tape.

Your live shot is about twenty minutes away. Do you air the shoot out as is—or do you edit out the portion of tape where people hit the ground after being shot? Some would argue that as a reporter you are the eyes and ears of the public; therefore, the public is entitled to see and hear the story as you heard and saw it unfold. Others would argue that you could use video and sound from the scene to tell the story just as well without subjecting your viewers to the gruesome nature of such a scene. Is there a right and wrong approach here? Not really. You may have an opinion or preference with respect to what should make air, but the final ruling on the question is in the hands of news administrators who may respectfully disagree with your assessment.

The trouble with breaking news in cases like this is that you have no idea how the story will end. Therefore, the decision to air or not to air material is sometimes out of your hands. Let's use the same scene, only this time assume your live shot is taking place just as the gunfire erupts.

Anchor: Good evening ... police are surrounding the First National Bank branch on the city's south side. Several armed gunmen are holding hostages and are threatening to kill them if their demands are not met. Let's go live to reporter Amanda Houston who is on the scene with the very latest.

Reporter: The situation began to unfold about an hour ago. You can see two of the gunmen at the entrance to the bank—one is aiming a weapon at police, the other at the head of a hostage.

At this point, one gunman begins shooting at police, the other shoots the hostage. Your station would never ordinarily allow this footage to be seen, but under these circumstances there is nothing that can be done. In future versions of this story, footage can be edited in such a fashion that no questionable video is used. In real-time television though, the policy guidelines are sometimes out the window.

In general, the news organization itself sets the parameters for what is tasteful and what is not. As a reporter, you can walk into a shop and quickly get a feel for the style of the station. It does not take long to figure out whether the station is conservative, "slash and trash," or somewhere in between when it comes to coverage. There is no clear-cut good or bad approach to presenting news. The presentation in many respects is market driven. If you consistently show viewers what they do not want to see, odds are pretty good that they will turn the channel and find another source for news. If a viewer finds your approach insensitive, he or she will be turned off and will, in turn, turn you off.

Balance in Coverage

Balance in coverage is another important area to discuss when talking about sensitivity. We have all heard that there are two sides to every story. The truth in many cases is that there are more, and in many reports there are less. As a reporter, it is one of your responsibilities to ensure that your piece is as balanced as it can be. This means seeking out opinion, reaction, expert analysis, and official comment when necessary and available. In many cases, this is easier said than done.

Your assignment is a six o'clock live report on an anti-abortion rally downtown. About fifty demonstrators will be opposing the planned opening of an abortion clinic in the area. Another fifty demonstrators will be there as well, to support the availability of such a facility. There are any number of ways to approach the story. Here, you are all but guaranteed interviews from individuals representing both sides of the debate. Your responsibility is to craft a presentation which presents a level look at the issue.

Unfortunately, not all stories present all sides at the same time or location. You may find ample information and interview subjects representing one side of the story at the scene, but be unable to get reactions or comments from the other side (or sides) at the time. This is typically the case in situations involving police actions and legal cases.

Scene: A city police officer shot and killed a young boy. The shooting occurred in a neighborhood where tensions between police and residents were already high. Police have secured the scene but are not talking to the press about what happened. Residents, on the other hand, are talking. One resident tells you the cop shot the kid in the head for no reason. Another said the youngster was unarmed and was playing with other kids when the officer opened fire for no apparent reason. A third "witness" tells you that the officer in question doesn't like people in this area and had threatened in the past to shoot someone. Police have called a news conference for seven o'clock to discuss the shooting. You are live at six. How do you craft a presentation that is balanced in this case when most of what you have weighs heavily against the officer and the police department?

Anchor: Good Evening ... a young boy is dead tonight after being shot by a city police officer. The shooting happened around five this evening, and right now there are a lot more questions than answers. We go live to reporter Amanda Houston on the scene for the latest.

Reporter: What we do know is that the youngster is thirteen years old. He was shot in the head by a police officer. What is unclear at this point is what prompted the shooting. Tensions between police and residents here have been on the rise for months now. Some residents tell me that the boy was unarmed and playing with friends when the shooting occurred. Another witness says the officer in question didn't get along with some in this area.

At this point "in this area" is the roll cue to the interview from that third witness. After the sound, the reporter is back on camera live to explain what the police are or are not saying and what is next.

Reporter: Police have yet to make any comment on the shooting. The police chief has called a seven o'clock news conference to discuss the matter. At that time I will ask him about some of the allegations made by residents here. Reporting from the scene, I'm Amanda Houston. Back to you in the studio.

Ideally, in this case you would have the chief on the scene where he could immediately respond to the allegations and give the officer's side of the story. Unfortunately, that has to wait. All you can do in this case is relate the few facts that you have and tell viewers what residents are saying about the situation. Two things are key here. One, you must make sure to attribute residents' comments to the residents. Failure to do so may make it appear that what you are saying and what they are saying is fact. The truth is, it might be, or it might not be. All we know for sure at this point is that a police officer shot and killed a child here. The second point is to let people know why there is no interview with a representative from the police department. You must explain the circumstances and assure them that you are pursuing all information on this case.

The danger in live situations where the ideal balance is hard to come by initially is that the reporter will engage in speculation to help fill out the story or fill time. This is can be a very dangerous practice. Your job in a case is simply to report the facts as you know them to be and to present all of the information available at that point. It is not your place to guess why something may have occurred or to draw conclusions from a handful of pieces to a complex puzzle.

Racism

Racism is without question one of the most significant issues facing our society today. It makes sense, then, that racial sensitivity in news coverage is a key concern in newsrooms around the country. Race-related sensitivity issues touch everything from the decision to cover a story, to how that story is covered, to who is behind the presentation. The live television news reporter must be keenly aware of all the concerns and issues he or she will encounter. Often, however, a reporter unknowingly offends without intending to do so. Why? Because he or she lacks the education or knowledge of the community needed to avoid such mistakes.

Racial Stereotyping

Of particular concern is racial stereotyping. In many cases, a thoughtless remark or inappropriate video clip is enough to raise concern. However, in even the most basic of stories, questions about stereotyping and sensitivity can be raised.

> **Scene:** Two rapes have occurred in one neighborhood in the past twenty-four hours. Police believe the attacker in both cases is the same person. The department has no one in custody. Officers were able to interview the two victims, but the victims were unable to recall much in terms of fine detail about the attacker. Here is what police do know based on the victim interviews: The attacker is believed to be a black male. He stands between five foot seven and six feet tall. The man weighs between 175 and 200 pounds. He was last seen wearing a white tee shirt, blue jeans, and white shoes. There is no composite sketch available.

Do you relate all of this information in your live report? In many cases, that depends on where you are working. Think about the suspect description again for a minute. It is vague enough to describe tens of thousands of people in cities like New York, Chicago, and Los Angeles. For that reason, some news operations will not air this information. The thinking is that the vagueness is more than enough to unfairly cast suspicion on a large group of people. The policy in some newsrooms is to air suspect descriptions only if there is a composite sketch to go along with them, or if there is some unique identifying characteristic. For example, the suspect has a tattoo of an eagle on his forehead. The same is true with any race. If there is little more to report than the color and sex of an individual, there is little to report. The exception might be in a community where no racial balance exists. If the rape suspect is a white male in a community that is 99.9 percent black, skin color becomes an important detail—especially if no composite sketch is available. This philosophy often frustrates law enforcement officials who want to get any and all known information about the case out.

There are many stations that will go with whatever police give them. Some believe the information is important enough to warrant broadcast—even though it does little to narrow the field of potential suspects. Many times, the description is aired because the story is important, and there is little else in terms of detail available at the time.

Racial Identification

This leads us nicely into another area of concern: racial identification. Lets go back to the original description of the rape suspect. He is described as a black male. But is black the appropriate way to refer to the man or is "African American" the correct ethnic label. How about the "Hispanic" population in your community, many of whom prefer being called "Latino." And you can not forget about "Asians," many of whom do not appreciate being lumped into that broad category used to describe Chinese, Japanese, Taiwanese, and other groups of Asian origin.

This is where as a live reporter you must be in tune with the community from which he or she is reporting and with the people who are the subject the report. This can be challenging, but it is critical to draw the same cultural distinctions and to know the preferences of the people involved before picking up the microphone. Respecting the sensitivity of residents and understanding their feelings and desires helps you better understand who and what you are reporting on. This can only enhance your credibility as a reporter and the credibility of your news product.

As a reporter it is important to keep your eyes and ears open to sensitivity concerns and to maintain a nondefensive posture when it comes to critiques and input from others. You must learn to invite input from other people. In a diverse newsroom it is great to have people who will come to you with and for advice. For example, you might have someone who is African American come up to you and say, "I don't know if you caught this on the five o'clock live shot you did, but you used the word 'ghetto' in your report." The reporter might go on to explain why "ghetto" might be viewed as a stereotypical reference. It is important to have people say in a constructive fashion that you might be walking on the wrong side of the line in certain cases. As a reporter, you have to be able to listen to people and build a rapport with them so they will not afraid to tell you when you may have stepped on someone's toes. This will benefit everyone in the long run.

Many stories will elicit different opinions from different ethnic groups. We saw this clearly in the O.J. Simpson murder trial. In this and other cases, there are clearly a number of different perspectives and reasons for them. It is your job as a reporter to seek diversity in your story. This is not to say that for every piece you need to track down not only a white person, an African American, a Hispanic, and an Asian, but also a Catholic, a Jew, and an Atheist for good measure. The point is to recognize the value in diversity and to seek as much of it as possible. Remember, we are all affected very differently by the same thing at times. It is important for you to draw from every resource available in order to understand and communicate the best story possible to your viewers.

New Assignments

Racial concerns also exist within the newsroom itself. When it comes to who covers what, reporters can be typecast or stereotyping can occur. In some cases, reporters will be sent to cover stories because they are black or white or Hispanic or Asian. The "wisdom" here is that if the reporter "fits in," he or she might produce a better piece than another reporter.

Long-time TV newsman Greg Prather points out that nothing could be further from the truth.

> I think as an African American I am more sensitive
> to how the African American Community is covered.
> As a journalist, I end up doing a lot of stories that

pertain more to the whole community that to just the minority community. Having said that, early on in my career, there was a story at the black student union on one of our college campuses. I sent a white female reporter out to cover the story. She immediately asked me if I was better equipped to cover the story. I immediately said no. It's a story, go cover it. To me, as it should be, it was just a story. Certainly there are certain sensibilities a reporter can bring to a story because he or she relates to it a bit better. All reporters though must be able to handle all settings and cultural diversity issues. I was sent to the back woods of North Carolina early on in my career. A place where people like me, a black person, aren't seen that often. It's a story. I have been sent out to cover KKK rallies, where I was sure I was not welcomed by the host, but I did the story. You could argue that maybe we should not have women reporting on the streets at night because it is not as safe as it should be. I am [very] much, though, [on the side] of equality in coverage—remember a story is a story—a person is a person—a reporter is a reporter.

Libel

What you say in a live report can have a tremendous impact on many people. If your information is not accurate or is not presented properly, it can also have a big impact on your career and your station's bank account. There are a number of legal questions that may arise out of a report or scene. One of the most critical areas of the law and reporting is libel. One of the best sources of information on the subject for reporters and news directors comes from the Associated Press (AP). The issue is so important to reporters that I have received permission from the Associated Press to use a portion of its libel manual in this book. Take notes and realize that everything you say can and will be held against you if you aren't careful.

AP Libel Manual

Libel, Defenses and Privilege

Libel is injury to reputation.

Words, pictures, or cartoons that expose a person to public hatred, shame, disgrace or ridicule or induce an ill opinion of a person are libelous.

Actions for civil libel result mainly from news stories that allege crime, fraud, dishonesty, immoral or dishonorable conduct, or stories that defame the subject professionally, causing financial loss either personally or to a business.

There is only one complete and unconditional defense to a civil action for libel: that the facts stated are PROVABLY TRUE. (Note well that word, PROVABLY.) Quoting someone correctly is not enough. The important thing is to be able to satisfy a jury that the libelous statement is substantially correct.

A second important defense is PRIVILEGE. Privilege is one of two kinds—absolute and qualified.

Absolute privilege means that certain people in some circumstances can state, without fear of being sued for libel, material which may be false, malicious and damaging. These circumstances include judicial, legislative, public and official proceedings and the contents of most public records. The doctrine of absolute privilege is founded on the fact that on certain occasions the public interest requires that some individuals be exempted from legal liability for what they say.

Remarks by a member of a legislative body in the discharge of official duties are not actionable. Similarly, libelous statements made in the course of legal proceedings by participants are also absolutely privileged, if they are relevant to the issue. Statements containing defamatory matter may be absolutely privileged if publication is required by law.

The interests of society require that judicial, legislative and similar official proceedings be subject to public discussion. To that extent, the rights of the individual about whom damaging statements may be made are subordinated to what are deemed to be the interests of the community.

We have been talking about absolute privilege as it applies to participants in the types of proceedings described here.

As applied to the press, the courts generally have held that privilege is not absolute, but rather is qualified. That means that it can be lost or diluted by how the journalist handles the material.

Privilege can be lost if there are errors in the report of the hearing, or if the plaintiff can show malice on the part of the publication or broadcast outlet.

An exception: Broadcasters have absolute privilege to carry the broadcast statements of political candidates who are given air time under the "equal opportunity" rules.

The two key points are:

1. Does the material at issue come from a privileged circumstance or proceeding?
2. Is the report a fair and accurate summation?

Again, the absolute privilege legislators enjoy—they can not be sued, for example, for anything said on the floor of the legislature—affords total protection.

The journalist's protection is not as tight. But it is important and substantial and enables the press to report freely on many items of public interest which otherwise would have to go unreported.

The press has a qualified privilege to report that John Doe has been arrested for bank robbery. If the report is fair and accurate, there is no problem.

Statements made outside the court by police or a prosecutor or an attorney may not be privileged unless the circumstances indicate it is an official proceeding. However, some states do extend privilege to these statements if made by specified top officials.

Newspapers and broadcasters often carry accounts going beyond the narrow confines of what is stated in the official charges, taking the risk without malice because they feel the importance of the case and the public interest warrant doing so.

The source of such statements should be specified. Sometimes there are traps.

In New York and some other states, court rules provide that the papers filed in matrimonial actions are sealed and thus not open to inspection by the general public.

But sometimes litigants or their lawyers may slip a copy of the papers to reporters. Publication of the material is dangerous because often the litigants come to terms outside of court and the case never goes to trial. So privilege may never attach to the accusations made in the court papers.

In one such case, the vice president of a company filed suit alleging that he was fired because the newspaper published his wife's charges of infidelity. The newspaper responded that its report was a true and fair account of court proceedings. The New York Court of Appeals rejected that argument on grounds that the law makes details of marital cases secret because spatting spouses frequently make unfounded charges. The newspaper appealed to the Supreme Court of the United States. But it lost.

Unless some other privilege applies, there is a danger in carrying a report of court papers that are not available for public inspection by reason of law, court rule or court order directing that such papers be sealed.

As stated earlier, a fair and accurate report of public and official proceedings is privileged.

There has never been an exact legal definition of what constitutes an official proceeding. Some cases are obvious—trials, legislative sessions and hearings, etc.

Strictly speaking, conventions of private organizations are not "public and official proceedings" even though they may be forums for discussions of public questions. Hence, statements made on the floor of convention sessions or from speakers' platforms may not be privileged.

Statements made by the president of the United States or a governor in the course of executive proceedings have absolute privilege for the speaker, even if false or defamatory. However, this absolute privilege may not apply to statements having no relation to executive proceedings.

President Kennedy once was asked at a news conference what he was going to do about "two well-known security risks" in the State Department. The reporter gave names when the president asked for them. This was not privileged and many newspapers and radio stations did not carry them. The Associated Press did because it seemed in the public interest to report the incident fully. No suits resulted.

After a civil rights march, George Wallace, then governor of Alabama, appeared on a television show and said some of the marchers were members of Communist and Communist-front organizations. He gave some names, which newspapers carried. Some libel suits resulted.

The courts have ruled that publishing that a person is a Communist is libelous on its face if he is not a Communist.

The claimed charge that the plaintiff is a Nazi and a Communist is in the same category. ... The current effect of these statements is the decisive test. Whatever doubt there may have been in the past as to the opprobrious effect on the ordinary mind of such a change ... recent events and legislation make it manifest that to label an attorney a Communist or Nazi is to taint him with disrepute. *(Levy vs. Gelber, 175 Misc. 746).*

The fact that news comes from official sources does not eliminate the concern. To say that a high police official said means that you are making the accusation. A statement that a crime has been committed and that the police are holding someone for questioning is reasonably safe, because it is provably true. However, there are times when the nature of the crime or the prominence of those involved requires broader treatment. Under those circumstances, the safest guide is whatever past experience has shown as to the responsibility of the source. The source must be trustworthy and certain to stand behind the information given.

Repetition of Libel

In reporting the filing of a libel suit, can we report the content of the charge? By so doing, do we compound the libel, even though we quote from the legal complaint?

Ordinarily, a fair and impartial report of the contents of legal papers in a libel action filed in the office of the clerk of the court is privileged. However, many states do not extend privilege to the filing of court actions; in such a case there is no privilege until the case comes to trial or until some other judicial action takes place.

But we have found that it is safe, generally speaking, to repeat the libel in a story based on the filing of a suit.

Fair Comment and Criticism

The publication of defamatory matter that consists of comment and opinion as distinguished from fact, with reference to matters of public interest or importance, is covered by the defense of fair comment.

Of course, whatever facts are stated must be true.

The right of fair comment has been summarized as follows:

"Everyone has a right to comment on matters of public interest and concern, provided they do so fairly and with an honest purpose. Such comments or criticism are not libelous, however severe in their terms, unless they are written maliciously. Thus it has been held that books, prints, pictures and statuary publicly exhibited, and the architecture of public buildings, and actors and exhibitors are all the legitimate subjects of newspapers' criticism, and such criticism fairly and honestly made is not libelous, however strong terms of censure may be." *(Hoeppner vs. Dunkirk Pr. Co., 254N.Y.95).*

Criminal Libel

The publication of a libel may result in what is considered a breach of the peace. For that reason, it may constitute a criminal offense. It is unnecessary to review that phase of the law here because the fundamental elements of the crime do not differ substantially from those that give rise to a civil action for damages.

Public Officials, Public Figures, Public Issues

In a series of decisions commencing in 1964, the Supreme Court established important First Amendment protections for the press in the libel area.

But in more recent decisions, the tide in libel has been running against the press, particularly in the unrelenting narrowing of the definition of a public figure. This was the single most active area of libel law in the decade of the '70s.

While the full impact of the later decisions is not yet clear, a review of the rulings since the mid-1960's shows the trend.

Three basic cases established important precedents. They did so in a logical progression. The cases were:

- New York Times vs. Sullivan (1964)
- Associated Press vs. Walker (1967)
- Gertz vs. Robert Welch (1974).

In The New York Times case, the Supreme Court ruled in March 1964 that public officials cannot recover damages for a report related to official duties unless they prove actual malice.

To establish actual malice, the official was required to prove that at the time of publication, those responsible for the story knew it was false or published it with reckless disregard of whether it was true or false.

The decision reversed a $500,000 libel verdict returned in Alabama against The New York Times and four black ministers. The court said:

"The constitutional guarantees (the First and Fourteenth Amendments) require, we think, a federal rule that prohibits a public official from recovering damages for a defamatory false-hood relating to his official conduct unless he proves that the statement was made with 'actual malice'—that is, with knowl-edge that it was false or with reckless disregard of whether it was false or not."

This does not give newspapers absolute immunity against libel suits by officials who are criticized. But it does mean that when a newspaper publishes information about a public official and publishes it without actual malice, it should be spared a damage suit even though some of the information may be wrong.

The court said it considered the case "against the back-ground of a profound national commitment to the principle that debate on public issues should be uninhibited, robust, and wide open, and that it may well include vehement, caustic and sometimes unpleasantly sharp attacks on government and public officials."

The ruling in The New York Times case with respect to public officials was extended by the Supreme Court in June 1967 to apply also to public figures.

In so holding, the court reversed a $500,000 libel judgment won by former Maj. Gen. Edwin A. Walker in a Texas state court against The Associated Press.

The AP reported that Walker had "assumed command" of

rioters at the University of Mississippi and "led a charge of students against federal marshals" when James H. Meredith was admitted to the university in September 1962. Walker alleged those statements to be false.

The court said: "Under any reasoning, Gen. Walker was a public man in whose public conduct society and the press had a legitimate and substantial interest."

The rulings in The New York Times and The Associated Press cases were constitutional landmark decisions for freedom of the press and speech. They offered safeguards not previously defined. But they did not confer license for defamatory statements or for reckless disregard for the truth.

The AP decision made an additional important distinction.

In the same opinion, the court upheld an award granted Wallace Butts, former athletic director of the University of Georgia, against Curtis Publishing Co. The suit was based on an article in the Saturday Evening Post accusing Butts of giving his football team's strategy secrets to an opposing coach prior to a game between the two schools.

The court found that Butts was a public figure, but said there was a substantial difference between the two cases. Justice Harlan said: "The evidence showed that the Butts story was in no sense 'hot news' and the editors of the magazine recognized the need for a thorough investigation of the serious charges. Elementary precautions were, nevertheless, ignored."

Chief Justice Warren, in a concurring opinion, referred to "slipshod and sketchy investigatory techniques employed to check the veracity of the source." He said the evidence disclosed "reckless disregard for the truth."

The differing rulings in The Associated Press and the Saturday Evening Post cases should be noted carefully. The AP-Walker case was "hot news"; the Post-Butts story was investigative reporting of which journalists are doing more and more.

Extension of the Times rule in one case was based on a column by Drew Pearson which characterized a candidate for the United States Senate as "a former small-time bootlegger." The jury held that the accusation related to the private sector of the candidate's life. Reversing this judgment, the Supreme Court said:

"We therefore hold as a matter of constitutional law that a charge of criminal conduct, no matter how remote in time or place, can never be irrelevant to an official's or a candidate's fitness for office for purposes of application of the 'knowing falsehood or reckless disregard' rule of New York Times vs. Sullivan."

Another case was brought by a Chicago captain of detectives against Time magazine, which had quoted from a report of the U.S. Civil Rights Commission without making clear that the charges of police brutality were those of the complainant whose home was raided and not the independent findings of the commission. The court described the commission's document as "bristling with ambiguities" and said Time did not engage in a "falsification" sufficient to sustain a finding of actual malice.

The progression of the New York Times, AP and Metromedia cases was interrupted in June 1974 with the Supreme Court's decision in the case of Gertz vs. Robert Welch Inc.

Gertz, a lawyer of prominence in Chicago, had been attacked in a John Birch Society publication as a Communist. There were additional accusations as well.

Gertz sued and the Supreme Court upheld him, ruling that he was neither a public official nor a public figure.

The decision opened the door to giving courts somewhat wider leeway in determining whether someone was a public person.

This case also opened the way to giving state courts the right to assess what standard of liability should be used in testing whether a publication about a private individual is actionable. It insisted, however, that some degree of fault, at least negligence, be shown.

For instance, some state courts have established a negligence standard (whether a reasonable person would have done the same thing as the publisher under the circumstances). The New York courts follow a gross negligence test. Others still observe the actual malice test in suits by private individuals against the press.

Bear in mind that the significance of the Gertz decision still is being developed, as new cases arise and are adjudicated. But at a minimum it opened the way to judgments the three earlier cases would seem to have barred.

More recently, in the case of Time vs. Firestone, the Supreme Court again appears to have restricted the public figure and the public issue standards.

The case stemmed from Time magazine's account of the divorce of Russell and Mary Alice Firestone. The magazine said she had been divorced on grounds of "extreme cruelty and adultery." The court made no finding on adultery. She sued.

She was a prominent social figure in Palm Beach, Fla., and held press conferences in the course of the divorce proceedings. Yet the Supreme Court said she was not a public figure because "she did not assume any role of special prominence in the affairs of society, other than perhaps Palm Beach society, and she did not thrust herself to the forefront of any particular public controversy in order to influence resolution of the issues involved in it."

As in the Gertz case, the decision opened the way to findings within the states involving negligence, a standard less severe than the actual malice standard that was at the base of three earlier landmark cases.

Supreme Court decisions, starting with Gertz and extending through Firestone and more recent cases, have consistently narrowed the class of persons to be treated as public figures under the Times-Sullivan and AP-Walker standards.

Two 1979 rulings by the Supreme Court illustrate the narrowing of the protections that seemed so wide only a few years earlier.

Sen. William Proxmire of Wisconsin was sued for $8 million by Ronald Hutchinson, a research scientist who had received several public grants, including one for $50,000. Proxmire gave Hutchinson a "Golden Fleece" award, saying Hutchinson "has made a fortune from his monkeys and in the process made a monkey of the American taxpayer." Hutchinson sued. The Supreme Court found that, despite the receipt of substantial public funds, Hutchinson was not a public figure. The court also ruled that Proxmire's news release was not protected by Congressional immunity.

Ilya Wolston pleaded guilty in 1957 to criminal contempt for failing to appear before a grand jury investigating espionage. A book published in 1974 referred to these events. Wolston alleged that he had been libeled. In ruling on Wolston vs. Reader's Digest, the Supreme Court said that he was not a public figure. The court said people convicted of crimes do not automatically become public figures. Wolston, the court said, was thrust into the public spotlight unwillingly.

In effect, the court extended the Firestone concept of un-willing notoriety to criminal as well as civil cases.

Thus the pattern through Gertz, Firestone, Proxmire and Reader's Digest is clear. The Times rule has been left standing but it is tougher and tougher to get in under it.

The court is rejecting the notion that a person can be a public figure simply because of the events that led to the story at issue. The courts are saying that public figure means people who seek the limelight, who inject themselves into public de-bate, etc. The courts are saying that involvement in a crime, even a newsworthy one, does not make one a public figure.

This means that the broad "public official" and "public fig-ure" protections that came out of the Times and AP cases re-main, but for shrinking numbers of people that are written about.

At the same time, the "reckless disregard of the truth" and "knowing falsity" standards of the Times decision also slip away, becoming applicable to fewer people as the public figure definition narrows.

And those standards are being replaced in state after state with simple negligence standards. In other words, the plaintiff, now adjudged to be a private citizen because of the recent rul-ings, must now prove only that the press was negligent, not reckless.

The difference is more than semantic. This development suggests that press lawyers will be relying more on some of the old standbys as defenses—plaintiff's inability to prove fal-sity, privilege, fair comment—and this puts the ball right back with editors and reporters.

The Supreme Court in 1986 held, however, in Philadelphia

Newspapers vs. Hepps, that, at least where a newspaper has published statements on a matter of public concern, a private figure plaintiff cannot prevail without showing the statements at issue are false. This case provides that the common law rule requiring a defendant to prove truth is supplanted by a constitutional requirement that the plaintiff demonstrate falsity when the statements involved are of public concern.

Another recent Supreme Court decision which provoked wide press controversy came in the case of Herbert vs. Lando.

The court ruled in 1979 that retired Army Lt. Col. Anthony Herbert, a Vietnam veteran, had the right to inquire into the editing process of a CBS "60 Minutes" segment, produced by Barry Lando, which provoked his suit. Herbert had claimed the right to do this so that he could establish actual malice.

The decision formalizes and calls attention to something that was at least implicit in the Times case, namely, that a plaintiff had the right to try to prove the press was reckless or even knew that what it was printing was a lie. How else could this be done except through inquiry about a reporter's or editor's state of mind?

So the ruling reminds plaintiffs' lawyers that they can do this and will, no doubt, be responsible for far more of this kind of inquiry than the press has had to face before.

A crucial test will be how far judges will let plaintiffs' lawyers range in their discovery efforts. Will they let the plaintiff widen the embrace of inquiry into stories other than the one at issue? Will they let the plaintiff rummage about the newsroom, probing unrelated news judgments, examining the handling of other unrelated stories, demanding to know why this investigative piece survived while that one died quietly on the kill hook?

That the questions are being prompted by the Herbert-

Lando ruling is the best response to those who say that the decision didn't really mean much.

The preliminary answer to these questions appears to be that there has been some widening of this sort of inquiry by plaintiffs newly alerted to this area by the Lando ruling. The press should be certain that files include contemporaneous memorandums that will testify later to the care taken with the story and the conviction that it was true and fair.

There was a footnote in the Proxmire case which has had a marked effect on the way libel cases are litigated. Footnote 9 questioned the practice of dismissing libel actions early in the course of litigation. The lower courts have paid serious attention to this footnote, with the result that more and more libel actions are being tried before a jury.

In a 1986 decision, Anderson vs. Liberty Lobby, however, the Supreme Court held that summary judgment should be granted in libel actions against public officials and public figures unless the plaintiff can probe actual malice with "convincing clarity" or by "clear and convincing evidence." This rule should facilitate the early dismissal of unmeritorious claims without the expense and burden of proceeding to trial.

The huge jury verdicts which often result have caused much concern among legal commentators and the press. A number of remedies have been proposed, but it remains unclear at this point whether the Supreme Court will take any action to stem the tide of runaway million-dollar jury verdicts of recent years. An indication that the Supreme Court is facing this problem appeared in its 1984 opinion in Bose vs. Consumers Union. Bose Corp. sued Consumer Reports over its publication of disparaging comments concerning Bose's loudspeaker systems and obtained a damage judgment of about $211,000. The Court of Appeals, after a careful review of the record, reversed. The Supreme Court endorsed this process, underscoring the need for appellate courts in libel cases to make an independent review of the record—a standard of scrutiny that does not apply in most other appeals. For the foreseeable future, the press will continue to rely on the willingness of the appeals courts to overturn excessive jury verdicts.

Summary of First Amendment Rules

The gist of the principles established in the cases discussed above may be summarized as follows:

A. The Public Official Rule: the press enjoys a great protection when it covers the affairs of public officials. In order to successfully sue for libel, a public official must prove actual malice. This means the public official must prove that the editor or reporter had knowledge that the facts were false or acted with reckless disregard for the truth.

B. The Public Figure Rule: the rule is the same for public figures and public officials. That is, a public figure must prove actual malice. The problem is that it is very difficult in many cases to predict who will be classified as a public figure. In general there are two types of public figures:

   1. General Purpose Public Figures: this is an individual who has assumed the role of special prominence in the affairs of society and occupies a position of persuasive power and influence. An example is the entertainer Johnny Carson.

   2. Limited Purpose Public Figures: this is a person who has thrust himself or herself into the vortex of a public controversy in an attempt to influence the resolution of the controversy. An example would be a vocal scientist who

has lectured and published articles in an attempt to influence a state legislature to ban fluoridation of water.

C. The Private Figure Rule: a private figure is defined in the negative. It is someone who is not a public figure. The rule of law for libel suits brought by private figures varies from state to state. The variations fall into three general categories:

1. A number of states follow the same rule for private figures and public figures. They require private figures to prove actual malice. These states include Alaska, Colorado, Indiana and Michigan.

2. One state, New York, requires private figures to prove that the publisher acted in a "grossly irresponsible manner." To date, no other state has adopted this rule.

3. Most states require private figures to prove only negligence. Negligence is a term of art which is difficult to define. As a rule of thumb, a careless error on the part of the journalist will often be found to constitute negligence.

These distinctions become important after the story has moved on our wires when there is a challenge and we are preparing our legal defenses. These distinctions do not apply in our preparation of stories. We do not have a standard that lets us go easier with ourselves if the story concerns a public official/figure and be tougher on ourselves if it concerns a private figure.

9

Resources

This is the live television news reporter's resource chapter. The information contained in this chapter is designed for use by both students and practitioners. Included in the chapter are two codes of ethics widely used in the industry and a list of numerically ranked television markets. This chapter also features the most comprehensive listing of television news and related internet sites available in one location.

Codes of Ethics

We will begin with two very important journalistic documents. These are the codes of ethics from the Radio-Television News Directors Association (RTNDA) and the Society of Professional Journalists (SPJ). Both present the guidelines for the coverage and reporting of news in an ethical, independent, and responsible fashion. If there are words to live by in this field, they are contained in these codes. Read them again and again. Support the organizations that hold these principles and standards in the highest regard.

RTNDA Code of Ethics

The responsibility of radio and television journalists is to gather and report information of importance and interest to the public accurately, honestly, and impartially.

The members of the Radio-Television News Directors Association accept these standards and will:

1. Strive to present the source or nature of broadcast news material in a way that is balanced, accurate and fair.
   A. They will evaluate information solely on its merits as news, rejecting sensationalism or misleading emphasis in any form.
   B. They will guard against using audio or video material in a way that deceives the audience.
   C. They will not mislead the public by presenting as spontaneous news any material which is staged or rehearsed.
   D. They will identify people by race, creed, nationality or prior status only when it is relevant.
   E. They will clearly label opinion and commentary.
   F. They will promptly acknowledge and correct errors.
2. Strive to conduct themselves in a manner that protects them from conflicts or interest, real or perceived. They will decline gifts or favors which would influence or appear to influence their judgments.
3. Respect the dignity, privacy and well-being of people with whom they deal.
4. Recognize the need to protect confidential sources. They will promise confidentiality only with the intention of keeping that promise.

5. Respect everyone's right to a fair trial.
6. Broadcast the private transmissions of other broadcasters only with permission.
7. Actively encourage observance of this Code by all journalists, whether members of the Radio-Television News Directors Association or not.

Unanimously Adopted by the RTNDA Board of Directors—August 31, 1987.

Reprinted by permission of the Radio-Television News Directors Association.

SPJ Code of Ethics
Preamble

Members of the Society of Professional Journalists believe that public enlightenment is the forerunner of justice and the foundation of democracy. The duty of the journalist is to further those ends by seeking truth and providing a fair and comprehensive account of events and issues. Conscientious journalists from all media and specialties strive to serve the public with thoroughness and honesty. Professional integrity is the cornerstone of a journalist's credibility.

Members of the Society share a dedication to ethical behavior and adopt this code to declare the Society's principles and standards of practice.

Seek Truth and Report It

Journalists should be honest, fair and courageous in gathering, reporting, and interpreting information. Journalists should:

- Test the accuracy of information from all sources and exercise care to avoid inadvertent error. Deliberate distortion is never permissible.
- Diligently seek out subjects of news stories to give them the opportunity to respond to allegations of wrongdoing.
- Identify sources whenever feasible. The public is entitled to as much information as possible on sources' reliability.
- Always question . sources' motives before promising anonymity. Clarify conditions attached to any promise made in exchange for information. Keep promises.
- Make certain that headlines, news teases and promotional material, photos, video, audio, graphics, sound bites, and quotations do not misrepresent. They should not oversimplify or highlight incidents out of context.
- Never distort the content of news photos or video. Image enhancement for technical clarity is always permissible. Label montages and photo illustrations.
- Avoid misleading reenactments or staged news events. If reenactment is necessary to tell a story, label it.
- Avoid undercover or other surretitious methods of gathering information except when traditional open methods will not yield information vital to the public. Use of such methods should be explained as part of the story.
- Never plagiarize.
- Tell the story of the diversity and magnitude of the human experience boldly, even when it is unpopular to do so.
- Examine their own cultural values and avoid imposing those values on others.
- Avoid stereotyping by race, gender, age, religion, ethnicity, geography, sexual orientation, disability, physical appearance, or social status.

- Support the open exchange of views, even views they find repugnant.
- Give voice to the voiceless; official and unofficial sources of information can be equally valid.
- Distinguish between advocacy and news reporting. Analysis and commentary should be labeled and not misrepresent fact or context.
- Distinguish news from advertising and shun hybrids that blur the lines between the two.
- Recognize a special obligation to ensure that the public's business is conducted in the open and that government records are open to inspection.

Minimize Harm

Ethical journalists treat sources, subjects, and colleagues as human beings deserving of respect. Journalists should:

- Show compassion for those who may be affected adversely by news coverage. Use special sensitivity when dealing with children and inexperienced sources or subjects.
- Be sensitive when seeking or using interviews or photographs of those affected by tragedy or grief.
- Recognize that gathering and reporting information may cause harm or discomfort. Pursuit of the news is not a license for arrogance.
- Recognize that private people have a greater right to control information about themselves than do public officials and others who seek power, influence, or attention. Only an overriding public need can justify intrusion into anyone's privacy.

- Show good taste. Avoid pandering to lurid curiosity.
- Be cautious about identifying juvenile suspects or victims of sex crimes.
- Be judicious about naming criminal suspects before the formal filing of charges.
- Balance a criminal suspect's fair trial rights with the public's right to be informed.

Act Independently

Journalists should be free of obligation to any interest other than the public's right to know. Journalists should:

- Avoid conflicts of interest, real or perceived.
- Remain free of associations and activities that may compromise integrity or damage credibility.
- Refuse gifts, favors, fees, free travel, and special treatment and shun secondary employment, political involvement, public office, and service in community organizations if they compromise journalistic integrity.
- Disclose unavoidable conflicts.
- Be vigilant and courageous about holding those with power accountable.
- Deny favored treatment to advertisers and special interests and resist their pressure to influence news coverage.
- Be wary of sources offering information for favors or money; avoid bidding for news.

Be Accountable

Journalists are accountable to their readers, listeners, viewers, and each other. Journalists should:

- Clarify and explain news coverage and invite dialogue with the public over journalistic conduct.
- Encourage the public to voice grievances against the news media.
- Admit mistakes and correct them promptly.
- Expose unethical practices of journalists and the news media.
- Abide by the same high standards to which they hold others.

Sigma Delta Chi's first Code of Ethics was borrowed from the American Society of Newspaper Editors in 1926. In 1973, Sigma Delta Chi wrote its own code, which was revised in 1984 and 1987. The present version of the Society of Professional Journalists' Code of Ethics was adopted in September 1996.

Reprinted by Permission of the Society of Professional Journalists.

The Internet

In this day and age, the Internet is becoming one of the most important tools any journalist can have. More and more newsrooms across the country are going *online* with and for information. For the live television news reporter, it means instant access to facts, figures, and other important information that can enhance a story. It is also an important resource for finding more information about other stations, jobs, clubs, organizations, and support groups that can help you make the contacts needed to advance your career. The Internet also affords you an opportunity to see how other news organizations are presenting their product. Writing and style information is clear on most web sites. You are able to determine what is important to that news operation and what approach the station takes to coverage.

The following pages contain web site and link information to a host of important broadcast related sites. The goal is to give you a host of locations to begin searching for the information you need. Remember, web sites and locations change from time to time, and additional site information may be found by using any number of Internet search engines.

URL addresses are shown for most of the listings. Those not shown can be found using any available web search engine and one or a combination of location and name keywords. For example, use the keyword "TELEVISION, NEWS, (and city you are searching for)" and a listing should appear. In many cases, you may find sites by typing in the name of the organization or station for direct link information. You might also try related keywords for additional links: TELEVISION, NEWS, BROADCAST, JOURNALISM, RESOURCES, INVESTIGATIONS, EDUCATION.

Professional TV Organizations with Web Sites/Links

- AEJMC—Association for Education in Journalism and Mass Communication: http://www.aejmc.sc.edu/online/home.html/
- AES—Audio Engineering Society: http://www.aes.org/
- AFIS—Armed Forces Information Service
- AFRTS—Armed Forces Radio and Television Service

- AFTRA—American Federation of Television and Radio Artists: http://www.aftra.org/
- AMPAS—Academy of Motion Picture Arts and Sciences: http://www.AMPAS.org/
- APTS—Association of America's Public Television Stations: http://www.apts.org
- ATAS—Academy of Television Arts and Sciences
- BDA—Broadcast Design Association
- BEA—Broadcast Educational Association: http://www.bea.org/
- CPB—Corporation for Public Broadcasting: http://www.fcc.gov/
- DGA—Directors Guild of America: http://www.dga.org
- FCC—Federal Communications Commission: http://www.fcc.gov/
- HIP TV—Hispanic Independent Producers
- ICA—Indigenous Communications Association
- IRE—Investigative Reporters and Editors: http://www.ire.org/
- ITVA—International Television Association: http://www.itva.org/
- ITVS—Independent Television Service: http://www.itvs.org/
- MIBTP—Minorities in Broadcasting Training Program
- MRC—Media Research Council: http://www.mrc.org/
- NAATA—National Asian American Telecommunications Association
- NAB—National Association of Broadcasters: http://www.nab.org

- NABET—National Association of Broadcast Employees and Technicians/CWA
- NABIPB—National Association of Blacks in Public Broadcasting
- NAHJ—National Association of Hispanic Journalists
- NAPBC—Native American Public Broadcasting Consortium, Inc.
- NFCB—National Federation of Community Broadcasters: http://www.nfcb.org/
- NHAMAS—National Hispanic Academy of Media Arts and Sciences
- NHMC—National Hispanic Media Coalition
- NLCC—National Latino Communications Center
- NPPA—National Press Photographers Association
- ONO—The Organization of News Ombudsmen: http://www.ono.org/
- PIC—Pacific Islanders in Communications
- RTNDA—Radio-Television News Directors Association: http://www.rtnda.org/
- SBE—Society of Broadcast Engineers: http://www.sbe.org/
- SMPTE—Society of Motion Picture and Television Engineers: http://www.smpte.org
- SOC—Society of Operating Cameramen: http://www.soc.org/
- SPJ—Society of Professional Journalists: http://www.spj.org/
- SSA—Small Station Association
- WICI—Women in Communication, Inc.
- WIFT—Women in Film and Television

Major TV Network Web Sites/Links

- ABC—American Broadcasting Company: http://www.abc.com/
- BBC Main WWW Site—(British Broadcasting)
- CBN—Christian Broadcasting Network
- CBS—Columbia Broadcasting System: http://www.cbs.com/
- CNBC—Consumer News and Business Channel
- CNN—Cable News Network: http://www.cnn.com
- C-SPAN
- ESPN SPORTS ZONE
- EWTN—Eternal World Television Network: http://www.ewtn.com/
- FOX—FOX Broadcasting Network: http://www.fox.com/
- MSNBC—Microsoft/NBC News: http://www.msnbc.com/
- NBC—National Broadcasting Company: http://www.nbc.com/
- PBS—Public Broadcasting Service: http://www.pbs.org/
- TELEMUNDO
- UNIVISION
- UPN—United Paramount Network: http://www.upn.com/
- VISN—Vision Interfaith Satellite Network
- WB—Warner Brothers: http://www.wb.com/

Local TV Station Web Sites/Links

- CLTV—Chicago, IL: http://www.cltv.com/

- KABB-TV—San Antonio, TX: http://www.kabb.com/
- KABC-TV—Los Angeles, CA
- KAET—Phoenix, AZ
- KAID-TV—Boise, ID
- KAMC-TV—Lubbock, TX
- KAMR-TV—Amarillo, TX: http://www.kamr.com/
- KARK-TV—Little Rock, AR: http://www.kark.com/
- KASN-TV—Little Rock, AR: http://www.kasn.com/
- KATU-TV—Portland, OR: http://www.katu.citysearch.com/local/
- KATV-TV—Little Rock, AR
- KBIA-TV—Columbia, MO
- KBJR-TV—Duluth, MN: http://www.kbjr.com/
- KBYU-TV—Provo, UT
- KCAL-TV—Los Angeles, CA
- KCBA-TV—Salinas, CA: http://www.kcba.com/
- KCBS-TV—Los Angeles, CA: http://www.kcbs.com/
- KCCI-TV—Des Moines, IA: http://www.kcci.com/
- KCNC-TV—Denver, CO: http://www.cbs.com/navbar/affiliates/
- KCRG-TV—Cedar Rapids, IA: http://www.kcrg.com/
- KCTV-TV—Kansas City, MO: http://www.kctv.com/
- KDFW-TV—Dallas-Ft. Worth, TX
- KDKA-TV—Pittsburgh, PA: http://www.kdka.com/
- KDLT-TV—Sioux Falls, SD
- KEPR-TV—Pasco, WA: http://www.keprtv.com/
- KERA-TV—Dallas–Ft. Worth, TX
- KETK-TV—Tyler, TX
- KEYE-TV—Austin, TX: http://www.k-eyetv.com/
- KFOR-TV—Oklahoma City, OK: http://www.kfor.com/

- KGAN-TV—Cedar Rapids, IA: http://www.2kgan.com/
- KGO-TV—San Francisco, CA
- KGTV-TV—San Diego, CA: http://www.abcnews.com/local/kgtv/
- KGW-TV—Portland, OR: http://www.kgw.com/
- KHON-TV—Honolulu, HI: http://www.khon.com/
- KHOU-TV—Houston, TX: http://www.khou.com/
- KHSL-TV—Chico-Redding, CA: http://www.khsltv.com/
- KISU-TV—Pocatello, ID
- KITU-TV—Beaumont, TX
- KITV-TV—Honolulu, HI: http://www.kitv.com/
- KIVI-TV—Boise, ID
- KJRH-TV—Tulsa, OK: http://www.kjrh.com/
- KJZZ-TV—Salt Lake City, UT: http://www.kzzj.com/
- KKTV-TV—Colorado Springs, CO: http://www.kktv.com/
- KLAS-TV—Las Vegas, NV: http://www.klas-tv.com/
- KLRT-TV—Little Rock, AR: http://www.klrt.com/
- KMBC-TV—Kansas City, MO: http://www.KMBC.com/
- KMGH-TV—Denver, CO: http://www.abcnews.com/local/kmgh/news/
- KMOL-TV—San Antonio, TX: http://www.kmol.com/
- KMSP-TV—Minneapolis–St. Paul, MN: http://www.kmsp.com/
- KNBC-TV—Burbank, CA
- KNOE-TV—Monroe, LA: http://www.knoe.com/
- KNTV-TV—San Jose, CA: http://www.kntv.com/

- KNVA-TV—Austin, TX: http://www.knva.com/
- KNXV-TV—Phoenix, AZ: http://www.knxv.com/
- KOAA-TV—Pueblo, CO: http://www.koaa.com/
- KOB-TV—Albuquerque, NM: http://www.kob.com/
- KOBI-TV, Medford, OR
- KOCO-TV—Oklahoma City, OK: http://www.kocotv.com/
- KOIN-TV—Portland, OR: http://www.koin.com/
- KOKH-TV—Oklahoma City, OK: http://www.kokh.com/
- KOLO-TV—Reno, NV: http://www.kolotv.com/
- KOLR-TV—Springfield, MO
- KOMO-TV—Seattle, WA: http://www.komotv.com/
- KOMU-TV—Columbia, MO: http://www.komu.com/
- KOTI-TV—Medford, OR
- KOVR-TV—Sacramento, CA: http://www.kovr.com/
- KPBS-TV—San Diego, CA
- KPDX-TV—Portland, OR: http://www.kpdx.com/
- KPIX-TV—San Francisco, CA: http://www.kpix.com/
- KPLC-TV—Lake Charles, LA
- KPTV-TV—Portland, OR
- KQED—San Francisco, CA
- KRBC-TV—Abilene, TX: http://www.krbctv.com/
- KRIS-TV—Corpus Christi, TX: http://www.kris.com/ (under construction)
- KRIV-TV—Houston, TX
- KRMA-TV—Denver, CO
- KSFY-TV—Sioux Falls, SD: http://www.ksfy.com/
- KSHB-TV—Kansas City, MO: http://www.kshb.com/
- KSL-TV—Salt Lake City, UT: http://www.ksl.com/tv/

- KSLA-TV—Shreveport, LA: http://www.ksla.com/
- KSNT-TV—Topeka, KS: http://www.ksnt.com/
- KSNW-TV—Wichita, KS
- KSSY-TV—Arroyo Grande, NM: http://www.kssy-tv.com/
- KSTU-TV—Salt Lake City, UT
- KTAB-TV—Abilene, TX: http://www.ktabtv.com/
- KTBS-TV—http://www.ktbs.com/
- KTFO-TV—Tulsa, OK
- KTIV-TV—Sioux City, IA: http://www.ktiv.com/
- KTLA-TV—Los Angeles, CA
- KTNV-TV—Las Vegas, NV: http://www.ktnv.com/
- KTRK-TV—Houston, TX
- KTSC-TV—Pueblo, CO
- KTVB-TV—Boise, ID: http://www.ktvb.com/
- KTVT-TV—Dallas–Ft. Worth, TX: http://www.ktvt.com/
- KTVX-TV—Salt Lake City, UT: http://www.ktvx.com/
- KTWU-TV—Topeka, KS
- KUAC-TV—Fairbanks, AK
- KUAT-TV—Tucson, AZ
- KUED-TV—Salt Lake City, UT
- KUHT-TV—Houston, TX
- KUID-TV—Moscow, ID
- KULR-TV—Billings, MT
- KUSA-TV—Denver, CO: http://www.kusa.com/
- KUSK-TV—Phoenix, AZ: http://www.kusk.com/
- KUSM-TV—Bozeman, MT
- KUTP-TV—Phoenix, AZ: http://www.kutp.com/
- KUTV-TV—Salt Lake City, UT: http://www.kutv.com/

- KVAL-TV—Eugene, OR: http://www.kval.com/
- KVBC-TV—Las Vegas, NV: http://www.kvbc.com/
- KVDA-TV—San Antonio, TX: http://www.kvda.com/
- KVIA-TV—El Paso, TX: http://www.kvia.com/
- KVIQ-TV—Eureka, CA: http://www.kviq.com/
- KVOA-TV—Tucson, AZ: http://www.kvoa.com/
- KVR-TV—Austin, TX
- KWTV-TV—Oklahoma City, OK: http://www.kwtv.com/
- KWWL-TV—Waterloo, Cedar Rapids, Dubuque, Iowa City, IA: http://www.kwwl.com/
- KXAN-TV—Austin, TX: http://www.kxan.com/
- KXAS-TV—Dallas-Ft. Worth: http://www.kxas.com/
- KXLY-TV—Spokane, WA: http://www.kxly.com/
- KXRM-TV—Colorado Springs, CO: http://www.kxrm.com
- KXTV-TV—Sacramento, CA
- KXTX-TV—Dallas, TX
- KYES-TV—Anchorage, AK: http://www.kyes.com/
- KYTV-TV—Springfield, MO

- WAAF-TV—Huntsville, AL
- WAAT-TV—Huntsville, AL
- WAAY-TV—Huntsville, AL: http://www.waay.com/
- WABC-TV—New York City, NY: http://www.abcnews.com/local/wabc/
- WABU-TV—Boston, MA
- WAGA-TV—Atlanta, GA: http://www.wagatv.com/
- WALA-TV—Mobile, AL
- WAND-TV—Decatur, IL: http://www.wandtv.com/

- WANE-TV—Ft. Wayne, IN: http://www.wane.com/
- WAVY-TV—Norfolk, VA: http://www.wavy.com/
- WBAL-TV—Baltimore, MD: http://www.wbaltv.com/
- WBBH-TV—Fort Meyers, FL: http://www.wbbhtv.com/
- WBBM-TV—Chicago, IL: http://www.cbs2chicago.com/
- WBC-TV—Columbus, IN
- WBGU-TV—Toledo, OH
- WBKO-TV—Bowling Green, KY: http://www.wbko.com/
- WBNX-TV—Cleveland, OH: http://www.wbnx.com/
- WBOC-TV—Salisbury, MD: http://www.wboc.com/
- WBRC-TV—Birmingham, AL: http://www.wbrc.com/
- WBRZ-TV—Baton Rouge, LA: http://www.wbrz.com/
- WBTV-TV—Charlotte, NC: http://www.wbtv.com/
- WBZ-TV—Boston, MA: http://www.wbz.com/
- WCAU-TV—Philadelphia, PA
- WCAX-TV—Burlington, VT: http://www.wcax.com/
- WCBS-TV—New York City, NY: http://www.wcbs-tv.com/
- WCCO-TV—Minneapolis, MN: http://www.wcco.com/
- WCET-TV—Cincinnati, OH
- WCIA-TV—Champaign-Urbana, IL: http://www.wcia.com/
- WCIV-TV—Charleston, SC: http://www.wciv.com/
- WCNC-TV—Charlotte, NC: http://www.wcnc.com/

- WCPO-TV—Cincinnati, OH: http://www.wcpo.com
- WCPX-TV—Orlando, FL: http://www.wcpx.com
- WCVB-TV—Boston, MA: http://www.wcvb.com
- WCYB-TV—Bristol, VA: http://www.wcyb.com
- WDAF-TV—Kansas City, MO
- WDBJ-TV—Roanoke, VA
- WDIV-TV—Detroit, MI: http://www.wdiv.com/
- WDJT-TV—Milwaukee, WI
- WDRB-TV—Louisville, KY: http://www.wdrb.com/
- WDTN-TV—Dayton, OH; http://www.wdtn.com/
- WDZL-TV—Hollywood, FL: http://www.wdzl.com/
- WEEK-TV—Peoria, IL: http://www.week.com/
- WEPT-TV—Community Television
- WETA-TV—Washington, DC
- WETV-TV—(Global Access—CANADA): http://www.wetv.com/
- WEVU-TV—Ft. Meyers–Naples, FL: http://www.wevutv.com
- WEVV-TV—Evansville, IN: http://www.wevv.com
- WFAA-TV—Dallas, TX: http://www.wfaa.com/
- WFIE-TV—Evansville, IN
- WFLD-TV—Chicago, IL: http://www.foxchicago.com/
- WFMJ-TV—Youngstown, OH: http://www.wfmj.com/
- WFMZ-TV—Allentown, PA: http://www.wfmz.com/
- WFRV-TV—Green Bay, WI: http://www.wfrv.com/
- WFSB-TV—Hartford, CT: http://www.wfsb.com/
- WFSU-TV—Tallahassee, FL
- WFTC-TV—Minneapolis, MN: http://www.wftc.com/

- WFTS-TV—Tampa, FL: http://www.wfts.com/
- WFTV-TV—Orlando, FL: http://www.wftv.com/
- WGBA-TV—Green Bay, WI: http://www.wgba.com
- WGBH-TV—Boston, MA
- WGBX-TV—Boston, MA
- WGBY-TV—Springfield, MA
- WGEM-TV—Quincy, IL
- WGN-TV—Chicago, IL: http://www.wgntv.com/
- WHA-TV—Wisconsin Public/Madison, WI
- WHAG-TV—Hagerstown, MD
- WHDH-TV—Boston, MA: http://www.whdh.com/
- WHEC-TV—Rochester, NY: http://www.whec.com/
- WHKY-TV—Hickory, NC: http://www.whky.com/
- WHNT-TV—Huntsville, AL
- WHO-TV—Des Moines, IA: http://www.who.com/
- WHRO-TV—Norfolk, VA
- WHYY-TV—Philadelphia, PA
- WILL-TV—Champaign-Urbana, IL
- WISC-TV—Madison, WI
- WISH-TV—Indianapolis, IN: http:// www.wishtv.com/
- WITI-TV—Milwaukee, WI
- WIVB-TV—Buffalo, NY: http://www.wivb.com/
- WJAC-TV—Johnstown, PA: http://www.wjactv.com/
- WJHG-TV—Panama City, FL
- WJHL-TV—Johnson City, TN: http:// www.wjhl.com/
- WJLA-TV—Washington, DC: http://www.wjla.com/
- WJXT-TV—Jacksonville, FL: http://www.wjxt.com/
- WJZ-TV—Baltimore, MD: http://www.wjz.com/
- WKAR-TV—East Lansing, MI

- WKBW-TV—Buffalo, NY: http://www.wkbw.com/
- WKPT-TV—Kingsport, TN: http://www.wkpttv.com/
- WKRG-TV—Mobile, AL: http://www.wkrg.com/
- WLBT-TV—Jackson, MS: http://www.wlbt.com/
- WLEX-TV—Lexington, KY: http://www.wlextv.com/
- WLKY-TV—Louisville, KY: http://www.wlky.com/
- WLNS-TV—Lansing, MI: http://www.wlns.com/
- WLOX-TV—Biloxi, MS: http://www.wlox.com/
- WLRN-TV—Miami, FL
- WLS-TV—Chicago, IL: http://www.abcnews.go.com/local/wls/
- WLUC-TV—Marquette, MI
- WLWT-TV—Cincinnati, OH: http://www.wlwt.com/
- WLXV-TV—Winston-Salem, NC
- WMAQ-TV—Chicago, IL: http://www.nbc5chi.com/
- WMBD-TV—Peoria, IL: http://www.wmbd.com/
- WMC-TV—Memphis, TN
- WMFE-TV—Orlando, FL
- WMGM-TV—Atlantic City, NJ: http://www.wmgmtv.com/
- WMTV-TV—Madison, WI
- WNBC-TV—New York City, NY
- WNEM-TV—Saginaw, MI: http://www.wnem.com/
- WNEP-TV—Scranton/Wilkes-Barre, PA: http://www.wnep.com/
- WNET-TV—New York, NY
- WNPB-TV—West Virginia
- WNYT-TV—Albany, NY: http://www.wnyt.com/
- WOFL-TV—Orlando, FL: http://www.wofl.com/
- WOLO-TV—Columbia, SC: http://www.wolo.com/

- WOUB/WOUC-TV—Athens, OH
- WOWK-TV—Charleston-Huntington, WV: http://www.wowktv.com/
- WPBY-TV—Huntington, WV
- WPHL-TV—Philadelphia, PA: http://www.wphl.com/
- WPIX-TV—New York, NY: http://www.wpix.com/
- WPTA-TV—Fort Wayne, IN: http://www.wpta.com/
- WPVI-TV—Philadelphia, PA: http://www.abcnews.com/local/wpvi/
- WRAL-TV—Raleigh, NC: http://www.wraltv.com/
- WRC-TV—Washington, DC: http://www.wrc.com/
- WRGB-TV—Schenectady, NY: http://www.wrgb.com/
- WRTV-TV—Indianapolis, IN: http://www.abcnews.com/local/wrtv/
- WSAW-TV—Wausau, Wisconsin: http://www.wsaw.com/
- WSAZ-TV—Huntington, WV: http://www.wsaz.com/
- WSB-TV—Atlanta, GA: http://www.accessatlanta.com/wsbtv/
- WSBE-TV—Providence, RI
- WSFA-TV—Montgomery, AL: http://www.wsfa.com/
- WSFP-TV—Fort Meyers, FL
- WSMV-TV—Nashville, TN: http://www.wsmv.com/
- WSOC-TV—Charlotte, NC
- WSVN-TV—Miami, FL: http://www.wsvn.com/
- WTEN-TV—Albany, NY: http://www.wten.com/
- WTHR-TV—Indianapolis, IN: http://www.wthr.com/

- WTIU-TV—Bloomington, IN
- WTLH-TV—Tallahassee, FL
- WTNH-TV—Hartford–New Haven, CT: http://www.wtnh.com/
- WTOL-TV—Toledo, OH: http://www.wtol.com/
- WTRF-TV—Wheeling, WV: http://www.wtrf.com/
- WTTV-TV—Indianapolis, IN
- WTVC-TV—Chattanooga, TN: http://www.wtvc.com/
- WTVF-TV—Nashville, TN
- WTVI-TV—Charlotte, NC
- WTVJ-TV—Miami, FL: http://www.wtvj.com/
- WTXL-TV—Tallahassee, FL: http://www.wtxl.com/
- WUFT-TV—Gainsville, FL: http://www.wuft.com/
- WUHF-TV—Rochester, NY
- WUPW-TV—Toledo, OH: http://www.wupw.com/
- WVBT-TV—Portsmouth, VA: http://www.wvbt.com/
- WVEC-TV—Norfolk, VA: http://www.wvec.com/
- WVIR-TV—Charlottesville, VA: http://www.wvirtv.com/
- WVIT-TV—Hartford-New Haven, CT
- WVLA-TV—Baton Rouge, LA
- WWBT-TV—Richmond, VA
- WWMT-TV—Kalamazoo, MI: http://www.wwmt.com/
- WXII-TV—Winston-Salem, NC: http://www.wxii.com/
- WXIN-TV—Indianapolis, IN: http://www.wxin.com/
- WXLV-TV—Greensboro, NC: http://www.wxlv.com/
- WXMI-TV—Grand Rapids, Kalamazoo, Battle Creek, MI: http://www.wxmi.com/
- WYFF-TV—Greensville, SC: http://www.wyff.com/

- WYOU-TV—Wilkes-Barre, Scranton, PA: http://www.wyou.com/
- WZTV-TV—Nashville, TN
- WZVN-TV—Fort Meyers, FL: http://www.wzvntv.com/

Cable TV Channel Web Sites/Links

- AIN—American Independent Network
- ALN—American Law Network
- ANC—All News Channel: http://www.allnews.com/
- AT—Americas Talking
- A&E—Arts & Entertainment Network
- BET—Black Entertainment Television: http://www.betnetworks.com/
- BORDER TELEVISION
- BRAVO: http://www.bravotv.com
- CARTOON NETWORK: http://www.cartoonnetwork.com/
- CLASSIC SPORTS NETWORK: http://www.classicsports.com/
- CNBC—Consumer News & Business Channel: http://www.cnbc.com/
- CNN—Cable News Network: http://www.cnn.com/
- COURT TV: http://www.cnn.com/
- CPAC—Cable Parliamentary Channel
- C-SPAN: http://www.c-span.org/
- THE DISCOVERY CHANNEL: http://www.discovery.com/
- E!—Entertainment Television
- ENCORE
- ESPN: http://www.espn.sportszone.com/

- THE FILIPINO CHANNEL
- FISH TV NETWORK: http://www.fishland.com/fishtv/
- FNN—Financial News Network
- FX: http://www.fxtv.com/
- GOLF CHANNEL
- HGTV—Home and Garden Television: http://www.hgtv.com/
- HOME TEAM SPORTS
- IC—International Channel
- KBL
- THE LEARNING CHANNEL: http://www.learningchannel.com/
- LIFETIME: http://www.lifetimetv.com/
- ME/U—Mind Extension University
- MTV—Music Television: http://www.mtv.com/
- NASA TV
- NEW ENGLAND SPORTS NETWORK: http://www.nesn.com/
- NEWS TALK TELEVISION
- NICKELODEON: http://www.nick.com/
- NOSTALGIA CHANNEL
- OUTDOOR CHANNEL: http://www.outdoorchannel.com/
- OVATION—The Arts Network
- PRISM
- SCI-FI CHANNEL
- SPORTS CHANNEL: http://www.sportschannel.com/
- THE SPORTS NETWORK: http://www.sportsnetwork.com/

- TBS SUPERSTATION: http://www.tbssuperstation.com/
- TELEVISION FOOD NETWORK: http://www.ww1foodnetwork.com/webpages/foodnetwork/default.html
- TNT—Turner Network Television: http://www.tnt-tv.com/
- TRAVEL CHANNEL: http://www.travelchannel.com/
- USA NETWORK: http://www.usanetwork.com/
- THE WEATHER CHANNEL: http://www.weather.com/
- WINGSPAN

Reference Web Sites/Links

- AMERICAN NEWS SERVICE: http://www.americannews.com
- THE ASSOCIATED PRESS ON-LINE: http://www.latimes.com/home/news/aponline/
- AT&T 1-800 PHONE DIRECTORY: http://www.800directory.com/
- BARTLETT'S FAMILIAR QUOTATIONS: http://www.columbia.edu/acis/bartleby/bartlett/
- BRITANNICA ONLINE: http://www.britannica.com/
- CENTRAL SOURCE: http://www.telephonebook.com/index.html
- CENTRAL SOURCE YELLOW PAGES
- CHRISTIAN SCIENCE MONITOR: http://www.csmonitor.com/headlines/apfeed/apfeed.html/

- CITY SEARCH: http://www.citysearch.com
- DOCUMENTS IN THE NEWS: http://www.lib.umich.edu/libhome/documents.center/docnews.html
- ELECTRIC LIBRARY: http://www.elibrary.com/id/101/101
- E-MAIL ADDRESS FINDER: http://www.sunsite.oit.unc.edu/
- E-MAIL ADDRESS FINDER: http://www.four11.com/
- FEDERAL AVIATION ADMINISTRATION: http://www.faa.gov/
- THE INFORMATION SUPER LIBRARY (TM): http://www.superlibrary.com/
- INTERNATIONAL E-MAIL DIRECTORY: http://www.worldemail.com
- INTERNET NEWSROOM: http://www.dgsys.com
- JOURNALISM RESOURCES: http://www.cio.com/WebMaster/journalism.html
- LIBRARY OF CONGRESS: http://www.lcweb.loc.gov/
- MAP QUEST: http://www.mapquest.com/
- MEDIANET: www.infinet/ncew/medianet.html
- NASDAQ: http://www.nasdaq.com/
- NATIONAL PHONE DIRECTORY: http://www3.switchboard.com
- NATIONAL PRESS CLUB: http://www.npc.press.org/
- NATIONAL TRANSPORTATION SAFETY BOARD: http://www.ntsb.gov/
- NETGUIDE: http://www.netguide.com

- NEWS TRENDS: http://nif.www.media.mit.edu
- NEW YORK STOCK EXCHANGE: http:// www.nyse.com/
- PRESSLINK: http://corpweb.krmediastream.com/
- REPORTER'S INTERNET GUIDE: http:// www.crl.com/rig.html
- REPORTER'S INTERNET SURVIVAL GUIDE: http://www.qun.com/
- REUTERS: http://www.reuters.com
- ROGET'S THESAURUS: http:// www.thesaurus.com/
- STRUNK'S ELEMENTS OF STYLE: http:// www.columbia.edu/acis/bartleby/strunk
- TRIBNET RESOURCES: http://www.tribnet.com./ journ.html
- UNITED STATES POSTAL SERVICE: http:// www.usps.gov/
- VIRTUAL LIBRARY: http://www.w3.org/ hypertext/datasources/bysubject/overview.html
- VOICE OF AMERICA: gopher://gopher.voa.gov
- WEBSTERS: http://www.dictionary.com/
- THE WHITE HOUSE: http://www.whitehouse.gov/
- WORLD MEDIA LINK: http://www.dds.ul/
- WORLD WIDE YELLOW PAGES: http:// www.netmation.com/www/yelltl.html

Search Engines

- ALTA VISTA: http://www.altavista.digital.com
- EXCITE: http://www.excite.com
- GALAXY: http://www.galaxy.com
- HOTBOT: http://www.hotbot.com

- INFOSEEK: http://www.guide.infoseek.com
- INSANE SEARCH: http://www.cosmix.com/motherload/insane/
- LYCOS: http://www.lycos.cs.cmu.edu
- OPEN TEXT: http://www.opentext.com:8080
- SUPER SEARCH: http://www.webtaxi.com/taxi/busib.html
- WEBCRAWLER: http://webcrawler.com
- YAHOO: http://www.yahoo.com

Television Markets (Ranked Numerically)

1. New York, NY
2. Los Angeles, CA
3. Chicago, IL
4. Philadelphia, PA
5. San Francisco-Oakland-San Jose, CA
6. Boston, MA
7. Dallas-Ft. Worth, TX
8. Washington, DC/Hagerstown, MD
9. Detroit, MI
10. Atlanta, GA
11. Houston, TX
12. Seattle-Tacoma, WA
13. Cleveland, OH
14. Tampa-St. Petersburg-Sarasota, FL
15. Minneapolis-St. Paul, MN
16. Miami-Ft. Lauderdale, FL
17. Phoenix, AZ
18. Denver, CO
19. Pittsburgh, PA

20. Sacramento-Stockton-Modesto, CA
21. St. Louis, MO
22. Orlando-Daytona Beach-Melbourne, FL
23. Portland, OR
24. Baltimore, MD
25. Indianapolis, IN
26. San Diego, CA
27. Hartford-New Haven, CT
28. Charlotte, NC
29. Raleigh-Durham, NC
30. Nashville, TN
31. Milwaukee, WI
32. Cincinatti, OH
33. Kansas City, MO
34. Columbus, OH
35. Greenville-Spartanburg, SC/Asheville, NC
36. Salt Lake City, UT
37. San Antonio, TX
38. Grand Rapids-Kalamazoo-Battle Creek, MI
39. Birmingham, AL
40. Norfolk-Portsmouth-Newport News, VA
41. New Orleans, LA
42. Buffalo, NY
43. Memphis, TN
44. West Palm Beach-Fort Pierce, FL
45. Oaklahoma City, OK
46. Harrisburg-Lancaster-Lebanon-York, PA
47. Greensboro-High Point-Winston–Salem, NC
48. Louisville, KY
49. Albuquerque-Santa Fe, NM
50. Providence, RI/New Bedford, MA

51. Wilkes Barre-Scranton, PA
52. Jacksonville, FL/Brunswick, GA
53. Albany-Schnectady-Troy, NY
54. Dayton, OH
55. Fresno-Visalia, CA
56. Las Vegas, NV
57. Little Rock-Pine Bluff, AR
58. Charleston-Huntington, WV
59. Tulsa, OK
60. Austin, TX
61. Richmond-Petersburg, VA
62. Mobile, AL/Pensacola, FL
63. Knoxville,TN
64. Flint-Saginaw-Bay City, MI
65. Wichita-Hutchinson, KS
66. Toledo, OH
67. Lexington, KY
68. Roanoke-Lynchburg, VA
69. Green Bay-Appleton, WI
70. Des Moines-Ames, IA
71. Honolulu, HI
72. Spokane, WA
73. Omaha, NE
74. Syracuse, NY
75. Shreveport, LA
76. Paducah, KY/Cape Girardeau, MO/Harrisburg-Mt. Vernon, IL
77. Rochester, NY
78. Tucson, AZ
79. Springfield, MO
80. Portland-Auburn, ME

81. Huntsville-Decatur-Florence, AL
82. Champaign-Springfield-Decatur, IL
83. Ft. Myers-Naples, FL
84. Madison, WI
85. South Bend-Elkhart, IN
86. Columbia, SC
87. Chattanooga, TN
88. Cedar Rapids-Waterloo-Dubuque, IA
89. Jackson, MS
90. Davenport, IA/Rock Island-Moline, IL
91. Burlington, VT/Plattsburgh, NY
92. Tri-Cities, TN/VA
93. Johnstown-Altoona, PA
94. Colorado Springs-Pueblo, CO
95. Waco-Temple-Bryan, TX
96. Evansville, IN
97. Youngstown, OH
98. Baton Rouge, LA
99. El Paso, TX
100. Savannah, GA
101. Lincoln-Hastings-Kearney, NE
102. Harlingen-Weslaco-Brownsville-McAllen, TX
103. Ft. Wayne, IN
104. Springfield-Holyoke, MA
105. Greenville-New Bern-Washington, NC
106. Lansing, MI
107. Tyler-Longview, TX
108. Reno, NV
109. Sioux Falls-Mitchell, SD
110. Peoria-Bloomington, IL
111. Augusta, GA

112. Florence-Myrtle Beach, SC
113. Montgomery, AL
114. Tallahassee, FL/Thomasville, GA
115. Fargo-Valley City, ND
116. Santa Barbara-Santa Maria-San Luis Obispo, CA
117. Ft. Smith, AR
118. Traverse City-Cadillac, MI
119. Monterey-Salinas, CA
120. Charleston, SC
121. Eugene, OR
122. Macon, GA
123. Lafayette, LA
124. Yakima-Pasco-Richland-Kennewick, WA
125. Boise, ID
126. Amarillo, TX
127. Corpus Christi, TX
128. Columbus, GA
129. La Crosse-Eau Claire, WI
130. Bakersfield, CA
131. Columbus-Tupelo-West Point, MS
132. Chico-Redding, CA
133. Monroe, LA/El Dorado, AR
134. Rockford, IL
135. Duluth, MN/Superior, WI
136. Wausaw-Rhinelander, WI
137. Beaumont-Port Arthur, TX
138. Wheeling, WV/Steubenville, OH
139. Terra Haute, IN
140. Topeka, KS
141. Wichita Falls, TX/Lawton, OK
142. Erie, PA

143. Medford-Klamath Falls, OR
144. Sioux City, IA
145. Columbia-Jefferson City, MO
146. Joplin, MO/Pittsburg, KS
147. Lubbock, TX
148. Albany, GA
149. Bluefield-Beckley-Oak Hill, WV
150. Minot-Bismarck-Dickinson, ND
151. Odessa-Midland, TX
152. Wilmington, NC
153. Rochester, MN/Mason City, IA/Austin, MN
154. Binghamton, NY
155. Bangor, ME
156. Anchorage, AK
157. Panama City, FL
158. Biloxi-Gulfport, MS
159. Abilene-Sweetwater, TX
160. Palm Springs, CA
161. Sherman, TX/Ada, OK
162. Quincy, IL/Hannibal, MO/Keokuk, IA
163. Salisbury, MD
164. Clarksburg-Weston, WV
165. Gainesville, FL
166. Idaho Falls-Pocatello, ID
167. Hattiesburg-Laurel, MS
168. Utica, NY
169. Billings, MT
170. Missoula, MT
171. Elmira, NY
172. Dothan, AL
173. Alexandria, LA

174. Rapid City, SD
175. Watertown, NY
176. Yuma, AZ/El Centro, CA
177. Marquette, MI
178. Jonesboro, AR
179. Lake Charles, LA
180. Harrisonburg, VA
181. Greenwood-Greenville, MS
182. Bowling Green, KY
183. Meridian, MS
184. Jackson, TN
185. Great Falls, MT
186. Parkersburg, WV
187. Mankato, MN
188. Grand Junction-Montrose, CO
189. Twin Falls, ID
190. St. Joseph, MO
191. Eureka, CA
192. Butte-Bozeman, MT
193. Charlottesville, VA
194. Laredo, TX
195. San Angelo, TX
196. Cheyenne, WY/Scottsbluff, NE/Sterling, CO
197. Lafayette, IN
198. Ottumwa, IA/Kirksville, MO
199. Casper-Riverton, WY
200. Bend, OR
201. Lima, OH
202. Zanesville, OH
203. Fairbanks, AK
204. Victoria, TX

205. Presque Isle, ME
206. Juneau, AK
207. Helena, MT
208. Alpena, MI
209. North Platte, NE
210. Glendive, MT

Suggested Readings

Block, Mervin. 1994. *Broadcast Newswriting: The RTNDA Reference Guide*. Chicago: Bonus Books.

———. 1990. *Rewriting Network News*. Chicago: Bonus Books.

———. 1997. *Writing Broadcast News*. Chicago: Bonus Books.

Coates, Charles. 1994. *Professional's TV News Handbook*. Chicago: Bonus Books.

Goald, Robert S. 1994. *Behind the Scenes at the Local News*. Newton, Mass.: Focal Press.

Hausman, Carl. 1992. *Crafting News for Electronic Media: Reporting and Producing*. Belmont, Calif.: Wadsworth Publishing Company.

Hinds, Lynn Boyd. 1995. *Broadcasting the Local News: The Early Years of Pittsburgh's KDKA-TV*. State College: Pennsylvania State University Press.

Matelski, Marilyn J. 1991. *TV News Ethics* (electronic media guides). Newton, Mass.: Focal Press.

Orlik, Peter B. 1997. *The Electronic Media: An Introduction to the Profession, Second Edition*. Ames: Iowa State University Press.

Pearlmann, Donn. 1986. *Breaking into Broadcasting*. Chicago: Bonus Books.

Stone, Vernon. 1993. *Let's Talk Pay*. Chicago: Bonus Books.

The Associated Press Stylebook and Libel Manual. 1996. New York: Addison-Wesley.

White, Ray, 1989. *TV News: Building a Career in Broadcast Journalism*. Newton, Mass.: Focal Press.

Wulfemeyer, K. Tim. 1993. *Beginning Broadcast News, Third Edition*. Ames: Iowa State University Press.

———. 1995. *Radio-TV Newswriting: A Workbook*. Ames: Iowa State University Press.

Yorke, Ivor. 1997. *Basic TV Reporting* (media manuals). Newton, Mass.: Focal Press.